PIONEERS OF HIS PRESENCE

CHRIS BURNS

Pioneers of His Presence
© 2014 Chris Burns

ISBN-13: 978-1500507039 (print book)
This book is also available in e-book format at your favorite online e-book store.

All rights reserved. No part of this book may be reproduced in any form, except for brief quotations in printed reviews, without permission in writing from the publisher.

www.burnsministries.com

Unless otherwise noted, all Scripture is taken from Scripture taken from the NEW AMERICAN STANDARD BIBLE®, Copyright © 1960, 1962, 1963, 1968, 1971, 1972, 1973, 1975, 1977, 1995 by The Lockman Foundation. Used by permission. Scripture quotations marked (NLT) are taken from the Holy Bible, New Living Translation, copyright © 1996, 2004, 2007 by Tyndale House Foundation. Used by permission of Tyndale House Publishers, Inc., Carol Stream, Illinois 60188. All rights reserved. Scripture also taken from the New King James Version®. Copyright © 1982 by Thomas Nelson, Inc. Used by permission. All rights reserved.

Cover design by Jeremy Bardwell at www.bardwelldesign.com
Typesetting by Katherine Lloyd at www.TheDESKonline.com

*This book is dedicated to my wife and partner, Danielle.
You are the true pioneer of His presence.
Thank you for making our lives a resting place
for the presence of God.*

Contents

Part One: The Man

1. The Pioneer 9
2. Fruitful by Nature 15
3. God's Love Language 27
4. God's Order 35
5. Good Workers Are Good Lovers 43
6. The Master 49

Part Two: The Map

7. Unique and Provoking Presence 61
8. Barren Lands and Rivers in the Desert ... 71
9. Mount Zion's Key 81
10. Habitation of God's Presence 91
11. Discipling Nations in the Presence ... 99
12. Heavenly Ministry and Cornerstones ... 107
13. The Government of the Presence 117

Part Three: The Mission

14. Jesus, the Pioneer Missionary 127
15. Turn the World Upside Down 135
16. Living Ahead of Your Time as Priests ... 143
17. Presence Pioneers 153
18. Monastic Missionaries 159
19. The Baby among Us 165

Part One

The Man

Chapter 1

THE PIONEER

Inside every pioneer is the faint but unending song of hunger for the undiscovered. This tune plays on repeatedly in the soul of every trailblazer. They thrive in the journey because to them it is better to explore uncertainty than to rest comfortably in predictability. They are convicted with a command to discover and convinced that things can be better than they've ever known before. To the way-maker and pathfinder, heartache and disappointment are only stepping-stones to the promise. On the inside of a true pioneer beats a heart that doesn't understand the language of doubt; these hearts beat strong with the blood of hope.

There have always been pioneers who pushed the limits of what was possible. Pioneers who go into unexplored territory in search of a new land, looking to establish permanent settlement. Pioneers take the few resources they own, unfinished maps, and hearts full of faith to go into uncharted lands to find places where they can implant their own cultures and ways of life.

We read of their stories and are spurned on to do the same. It excites us to learn of the great adventurers of old who captivate our hearts with stories of discovering new things and new lands. And those starry-eyed wanderers who gave their all to seek out things not yet discovered.

From Marco Polo to Christopher Columbus, from the American frontiersmen to Neil Armstrong, there have always been pioneers who possess the inexplicable hunger to discover the undiscovered. Even the pioneers of medicine, invention, and the arts pushed up against common beliefs to attempt things only dreamed of. Where would we be without these wild-eyed dreamers? Without their discoveries, we would be in a completely different world than we now know.

But there is another type of forerunner who goes farther and deeper still. The heavenly pioneer.

These men and women are looking to change the world we live in, not by discovering new lands, new cures, or new good ideas, but by discovering more of the Creator Himself and bringing Him to earth. These pioneers have looked into eternity and heard the voice of the uncreated one. They seek to make this world look like His world, and they are possessed with the very presence of God.

These are the gateways between His world and ours. They are God's own, who deny religion's comfort and walk daringly into the fullness and mystery of God. The Bible is full of them. Hebrews 11 talks about some of these heroes of the faith. Church history resonates with the call to pioneer through the fathers and mothers who have gone before us.

> ... who through faith conquered kingdoms, administered justice, and gained what was promised; who shut the mouths of lions, quenched the fury of the flames, and escaped the edge of the sword; whose weakness was turned to strength; and who became powerful in battle and routed foreign armies. Women received back their dead, raised to life again. There were others who were

tortured, refusing to be released so that they might gain an even better resurrection. Some faced jeers and flogging, and even chains and imprisonment. They were put to death by stoning; they were sawed in two; they were killed by the sword. They went about in sheepskins and goatskins, destitute, persecuted and mistreated— the world was not worthy of them. They wandered in deserts and mountains, living in caves and in holes in the ground. These were all commended for their faith, yet none of them received what had been promised, since God had planned something better for us so that only together with us would they be made perfect. (Hebrews 11:33–40)

These pioneers were driven by an inward yearning for God and a desire to create a place for Him on the earth, to build something that had not yet been seen in a land not established. Like Father Abraham before them, they left comfort and predictability for a place they only knew by a glimmer of promise.

There have always been pioneers in the church, though few they may have been. They showed us ancient paths that led to fresh life and truth. Today, I believe another great wave of pioneering hearts has begun to hit the shores of this earth—perhaps more so than ever before in history.

For this reason, I seek to lay out a path, a map of sorts, to show us how to build in the coming years. If we build without knowing the Master's blueprint, we will have to live in a house that we never intended on living in. If we set sail without a compass, coordinates, and a map, we will end up in a place we never intended to be—like much of the church today. How can we build without knowing *what* we're building?

We are living in a time of history when we aren't afforded the luxury of wandering in the wilderness for decades. God is now wooing the church back to her first love, Jesus. He is establishing our foundation as Jesus, the very presence of God with us. He is changing the way the church does "business."

No longer will we succumb to doing the work and not knowing the Man. Gone are the days of being driven by the newest cunning schemes of how to do church; instead, we are driven by the mystery and power of His consuming presence. God wants a family, not an organization. And since worship and prayer are the language of intimacy with God, a prayer-and-worship movement is now sweeping the earth at unprecedented speed and size.

Churches all over the earth are starting to pray around the clock. Worship times are sabotaging the well-thought-out plans of men, and God is breaking in with His power. This movement is growing and accelerating by the day. It is multi-faceted, multi-cultural, and multi-generational. You may have not heard this on your favorite news channel, but if you tune in to the newscast of heaven, you will know that the Spirit of God is raising up a prayer-and-worship culture in the church like never before. This culture values real relationship with Jesus above all else. God in His great wisdom is luring the church back to Him in love through the joy and life found in His presence.

Houses of prayer and worship are being established in the earth, bringing the very throne of God to cities and nations across the world. Psalm 22:3 declares that "God sits enthroned in the praises of Israel." God inhabits and sets up His throne in the very midst of praise. He did it on the earth in King David's day. His manifest presence rested in the Tabernacle of David for thirty-three years, and He is doing the same in our day, but on a much grander scale.

The answer has, is, and always will be God's presence and

glory on the earth. We are the gateways from the heavenly realm to this world. We are citizens of heaven and ambassadors of the kingdom of God. We exist on the earth to love God as priests and carry His presence as kings. God is calling for "presence-carrying pioneers" in the earth today. He is awakening those who would pioneer the presence of God in cities and regions across the earth in places that are in deep darkness, void of the light of God's nearness. He is calling even the least of these to mine out a place where He can find rest, both in the human heart and in the high places of culture. There is no higher calling than to walk with God and to worship Him, and both high and low are being beckoned!

The presence of God is mysterious and yet very simple. We must not allow mystery to turn into complexity. In the Bible the one and only definition of the word *presence* is "face." The word for presence is *paniym* and every single time it means face. The presence of the Lord is the very face of God. It needs to be made clear that God is everywhere but not in everything. He is inside every born-again believer, but He is not seen *upon* every believer. His omnipresence and manifest presence are different. His presence can be seen with the right eyes in all of creation. But His face speaks of the very nearness of His person. God wants to give the world an encounter with His presence. He wants the world to see the beauty of His face and the nearness of His goodness.

We are called to carry His face and the beauty of who He is to the world while proclaiming the good news! We are on the earth to bring His kingdom. One thing must hold our constant attention: we are to implant the culture of heaven into every sphere of this world. Heaven is filled with His manifest presence and glory. We are to bring God's life-giving presence and all of its benefits to a world in need. We are from heaven, we were born of God, and our primary purpose in every act, great and small, is to bring His kingdom, His culture, and His way of life here.

You may be wondering, *Is the presence of God really the only thing we should be concerning ourselves with in the church today? Is this prayer-and-worship movement the only thing of importance?*

I say, "No. It is not the only thing. But it *is* the first thing."

The presence of God, knowing Him and Him knowing us, and living out a first-commandment lifestyle, is the foundation to everything we do. We do not graduate from intimacy; we only build on it. We do not get it right and then move on; we continually cultivate this in our individual and corporate lives. We do not simply come back to relationship with God every so often when we are dry; we live *out* of this place.

Let it be made clear: the first and greatest commandment is the foundation of all life: "To love the Lord God with all your heart, soul, mind and strength" (Matthew 22:36–37).

If we do not begin to pioneer His presence in our lives by living out a first-commandment lifestyle, we will fall depressingly short of our high calling in Christ. If we do not pioneer His presence in our homes, cities, and nations, we will reap a place that looks much like hell on earth, void of the light of His glory, thereby allowing darkness to have its way.

Pioneer, it is time to begin your work. I pray as you read the revelation from these pages that the word of God will strike your spirit like a flame and His presence will fuel you to go into the depths of His heart. As this language penetrates your spirit, know that you are responsible for what you hear and learn. May the blessing of revelation and wisdom be upon you!

Chapter 2

FRUITFUL BY NATURE

The most fruitful thing we can do in our lives is to abide in the presence of God. Just like the children of Israel in the wilderness whose very way of life revolved around God's presence, we too must come to the place of abiding in the presence as our supreme priority. As the children of Israel followed the presence of God and camped around it, they were led into new lands and nations where the presence of the Lord was not known. This is the calling of the church today. If we wish to do the same things, we must make abiding in His presence the "bull's-eye" of our lives. Jesus commands abiding for the sake of relationship, and He wants relationship so that fruitfulness can happen naturally.

> Abide in Me, and I in you. As the branch cannot bear fruit of itself unless it abides in the vine, so neither can you unless you abide in Me. I am the vine, you are the branches; he who abides in Me and I in him, he bears much fruit, for apart from Me you can do nothing. (John 15:4–5)

Bearing fruit is the identifying factor of a follower of Jesus. Jesus said we would *prove* to be His disciples by the fruit of our lives (John 15:8). It's not just what we say, how we act, and what we do that makes us followers of Jesus. We can say we follow Christ and live contrary to that statement. We can act like Christians and do the devil's will. We can even do miracles in the name of God yet have it count for nothing. If we do not have the first commandment as the pursuit of our lives and the basis of all we do, we will end up gaining the world yet losing our own souls (Mark 8:36), just like the "Lord, Lord" Christians in Matthew 7.

> Not everyone who says to Me, "Lord, Lord," shall enter the kingdom of heaven, but he who does the will of My Father in heaven. Many will say to Me in that day, "Lord, Lord, have we not prophesied in Your name, cast out demons in Your name, and done many wonders in Your name?" And then I will declare to them, "I never knew you; depart from Me, you who practice lawlessness!" (Matthew 7:21–23)

We can do the works and not know the Man. This is why fruit is different from good works. If good works alone were fruit, then we could do them and bear fruit without Jesus. Fruit that remains are works that are done *with* Him, not apart from Him. According to our Savior's words in John 15, it is impossible to bear fruit without living our lives in His presence (John 15:4–5). We cannot bear fruit without a relationship with Jesus. Many do good works apart from Jesus. Good works apart from the presence of God don't last. Paul makes it clear in 1 Corinthians 3:10–14 that all the "good" things we do that are not founded upon Jesus will be burned up and found to be good for nothing. In fact, the Bible says that our own good works and righteous deeds apart from God are as filthy rags (Isaiah 64:6).

Fruit bearing is less about *doing* and more about *abiding*. Abiding is more about *being* in God and He in us than it is about *doing* things to attain to a place with God. The natural overflow of a person who walks with God will be good works. As Paul said in Galatians 2:20, "It is no longer I who live but Christ living in me." It is Christ in us doing the work as we surrender to His leadership. The only way to bear fruit is to abide in Christ, to live and walk with Him and in His presence. To abide means to live or stay somewhere, or in this case, to live and stay in His presence. God's presence is the nearness of His person. We must live in the nearness of God through intimacy with Him. This is the only way to abide.

It is possible to think we are doing the works of God and miss His will completely. If our focus is on Him, it is hard to miss His will. But when our gaze becomes infatuated with the things of God and not God Himself, we are guaranteed to be unfruitful.

Fruit isn't just the presence of good works or righteous living. It means that people and the world around you are feeding from your life. The fruit in my life isn't for me; it's for others. Just like the anointing of the Holy Spirit or the gifts of God upon the believer, they are for the world around us. Jesus said His anointing was for others when He declared, "The Spirit of the Lord God is upon me because he anointed me to preach the gospel to the poor. He has sent me to proclaim release to the captives, and recovery of sight to the blind, to set free those who are oppressed" (Luke 4:18). Fruit, like the anointing of the Holy Spirit, is primarily for those we are called to serve.

The fruit of your life can be anything and everything—from the way you live as a witness to others, your words, your actions, etc. But one thing is for sure: the fruit you bear is for others. Just as Jesus was the bread of life and the water from heaven, we too are to be a source of life to those around us. We are to become "food" to the hungry souls we encounter every day. Our preaching doesn't bear fruit; it gives the fruit we have already grown. Our ministering to others doesn't bear fruit; it gives to others the fruit grown in intimacy with Jesus. Our fruit isn't for showing off; it is for eating. The fruit we give when ministering and serving, in whatever capacity, brings life to others; this is how we have fruit among people. But without living life in God, we have nothing real to give. Living in God's love for us, and our love for Him, is how Jesus taught us to bear fruit.

> My Father is glorified by this, that you bear much fruit, and so prove to be My disciples. Just as the Father has loved Me, I have also loved you; abide in My love. (John 15:8–9)

New Covenant Fruit

This is why living in a new-covenant, first-commandment lifestyle is so important. The first commandment is to love God with all your heart, soul, mind, and strength. The new covenant is not about how much we love God, but how much God loves us. This divine romance has its beginning in that He loved us first, initiating the relationship and making a way for it to become real. To live a new-covenant, first-commandment lifestyle means that the entirety of how we live revolves around daily knowing and experiencing His great love for us, and then reciprocating that love to Him in all we do.

The Bible makes clear a massive shift in man's relationship to God between the new and old covenant. The old covenant between God and man involved men basing their relationship with God on meeting certain requirements. While it wasn't evil in and of itself, it fell short of the fullness of true relationship, which is what God has always desired. The old covenant, or the old agreement or contract between God and man, showed us our inability to live in a way whereby we could abide in God. Even more so, it showed the inability of people to bring forth the real and lasting fruit of heaven. The mind-set of the old covenant church (the people of God in that time) was largely based on following the law. They thought that if they met all of God's requirements and did their best to follow every jot and tittle of the law, they would please God. But this covenant wasn't the fullness of God's plan. God wasn't after rule followers; His heart was seen between the lines of the Old Testament law. His heart was to have the love of His people. When we approach God trying to bear fruit in this way, we maintain the old-covenant mind-set and lose out on the joy of real relationship.

Jesus came to do many things, one of which was to restore us to God, not based on our works or worthiness but by His works and worthiness. The gospel of Jesus Christ brings us the new covenant. New-covenant thinking is based on abiding in relationship. There is nothing more important than living life with God. The law of following the Spirit is greater than the law of following the rules. Following and staying in relationship with God lead us in the greater way, a way that the law could not and never will show us. The Old Testament law was like knowing about God, whereas the New Testament shows us that we can know God personally—like the difference between reading a biography about someone and actually knowing the person. The new covenant restores "garden life" to God's people, and all mankind is invited into this relationship with Him. The blood of Jesus, the perfect Lamb and Son of God, was slain as our sacrifice so we could walk with God blameless. Just like the first people in the garden, our supreme goal and joy in life is that we can actually walk with God.

Jesus desires for the church to be fruitful, both individually and as a corporate body. His words to His followers then hold the same truth for us now.

> You did not choose Me but I chose you, and appointed you that you would go and bear fruit, and that your fruit would remain. (John 15:16)

Within this verse we peek into the heart of God and see a supreme desire of His heart for us. His desire for us is to bear fruit that remains. Our fruit is not to grow in certain seasons only. We are to be like a tree planted beside the water that bears fruit in and out of season (Psalm 1:3). This fruit must come from abiding in God, and it must have the essence of eternity upon it. All that God grows in us will have the stamp of divine and timeless impact.

> By faith we understand that the worlds were prepared by the word of God, so that what is seen was not made out of things which are visible. (Hebrews 11:3).

The unseen things create the seen things. God created everything we see by His word, which is unseen. The spiritual realm, which is unseen, has precedence over the natural realm. All things in this natural world are influenced by the spiritual world, the unseen place. Abiding in God happens within the interior of our lives: the secret meetings with God as well as the daily conversations and leadings of the Holy Spirit. You cannot see intimacy, as it is an unseen reality. Yet having intimacy with God will produce the things people *can* see. Sowing into the unseen place produces fruit that has been inspired by being connected to the very Word of God, who is Jesus Christ. His Word is eternal and will never pass away. This is why, when fruit grows from His word, it remains. This is why you can only have fruit if your connection to Him is strong and stays current day to day.

The Bible proclaims that the unseen is eternal and preeminent (2 Corinthians 4:18). As God's people upon the earth, we must live from that unseen place with God in order to bear fruit. If our works of righteousness are all in the "seen" places, we may think we have borne fruit. But let us not be deceived into thinking that we are fruitful people because of our public ministry successes.

Real and lasting fruit comes from a life given to the unseen place. The secret place of intimacy and abiding with God is how we bear fruit that remains. Fruitfulness can include fruitful works of ministry done in obedience to the leading and voice of God. Even the individual fruits of the Holy Spirit, like love, patience, and joy, come forth from a life lived in God. But without a life given to the unseen, no fruit will come forth.

When people eat, they are filled and their bodies are energized. The words Jesus spoke are spirit and life (John 6:63). His words always give life and energize our spirits. To be a fruitful tree means that even our most simplistic and everyday words and works give life and vitality to the world around us. Jesus solidifies this in His sermon at the beginning of Matthew 6. The secret place is a place of intimacy, and its ultimate end is outward reward. What you do in secret will be rewarded openly.

Look at the apple tree. The apple comes forth on the tree because of all the inner workings going on inside the tree. The apple is the overflow and natural producing of what that tree was made to do. The tree supplies all the things necessary for that apple to come forth and be seen. Our inner life of abiding with God is of much more value than outward ministry success. Outward success in the eyes of man can be misleading to the true condition of our relationship with God.

This idea can be offensive to our religious leanings. It is always easier to mark off a checklist of dos and don'ts than to get our hearts involved. But the latter is far more rewarding. God is after our hearts, not our service. The Lord does want obedience, but our good works for Him need not be in vain. Paul made it clear in 1 Corinthians 13 that without love, even our greatest works can be done in vain. God is love. Love is defined by the very nature of who God is. The Lord beckons us to get to know Him, because knowing Him is knowing true love. In His infinite wisdom He has designed it this way so that when He gets our hearts, he naturally gets our service. If we go after the heart of God in the secret place, He will reward us in the public place with fruitfulness that remains and that cannot be taken away. As in Matthew 6, the promise of His open rewards comes from secret service to Him. These rewards can't be stolen or eaten away by anything on the earth, because they were born in heaven. What a provoking promise to go deep in God!

Things Are Changing

When Jesus taught His disciples in John 15, He announced a return to a different set of ideals for those who follow God. This was also a return to garden living. It signified a return to walking with God as Adam and Eve did. Jesus was saying that the only way to bear fruit was to walk with Him in relationship. No other option. He leaves no alternatives for fruit production. This is an earth-shaking, revolutionary idea. He, being the Vine and speaking on behalf of the Head Gardener, says, "If you do not abide in me you will bear no fruit, if you abide in me and I in you will bear much fruit and fruit that remains."

In this passage of Scripture, Jesus was restoring the original design of God's intended relationship with man, so that we would change the world through abiding in relationship with Him, carrying out His will and good pleasure as in the garden.

Before man fell, we "walked in the cool of the day" (Genesis 3:8) with the Lord and bore fruit by being in relationship with God. This is what we are called to again—only the Lord did not put us back into the garden. Instead, He put the garden inside us. As we tend to this inner garden, our outside world begins to resemble the glory within.

In the fall of man in Genesis 3, the Lord said to Adam something interesting in regard to fruit and getting the earth to produce.

> Cursed is the ground because of you; In toil you will eat of it all the days of your life. Both thorns and thistles it shall grow for you; and you will eat the plants of the field; By the sweat of your face you will eat bread, till you return to the ground, because from it you were taken; for you are dust, and to dust you shall return. (Genesis 3:17–18)

This verse implies that what was once attained in the ease of His presence would now have to be earned and worked for. This is the first thing God said to Adam after sin came into the earth. At the fall of man, as the curse entered in, God told Adam that he would have to work by the sweat of his brow. No longer could Adam and his sons bring forth fruit simply by being with God and walking with Him in the cool of the day. The fruitfulness

Adam was bringing forth through relationship would now be done in large part through his own works.

When Jesus stepped on the scene and proclaimed His words in John 15, He changed the very roots of our religious endeavors. He released heaven's decree of a shift in the way of life for the follower of God. His declaration of this new-covenant reality says, "*Learn to dwell in the garden with me again! Abide, live, dwell, stay and engage with me always and you will bear life-giving fruit!*" No longer are we to toil and strive to meet the rules to bear fruit. Instead, we will bear fruit through the joys of relationship. What a freeing reality that God just wants to be with us, and if we give ourselves to Him in this way, He will change the world through us.

This is not to perpetuate or encourage the idea of sitting in God's presence and doing nothing. Bearing fruit happens in the prayer room, the workplace, the streets, and the pulpit as we simply commune with Jesus and are obedient to His commands. The issue comes when we try to do all these things without being in day-to-day relationship with God. Success in life or ministry is not an indicator of God's approval of our relationship to Him. Our focus should be on abiding, not on working or serving.

We do not bear fruit by doing ministry; we bear fruit by abiding in the Vine. Only by being with Jesus can we bear fruit. It is possible to serve God and not listen to Him or love Him. Martha of Bethany is a perfect example of this. Her serving the Lord had replaced her simple devotion of love and worship to Him (Luke 10:38–42). Her service was from the right heart, but she missed the greater thing: the greatest and first commandment, which is to love God. If we will come to know and daily experience God's love for us, we will daily abide in Him and bear fruit.

We have come to know and have believed the love which God has for us. God is love, and the one who abides in love abides in God, and God abides in him. (1 John 4:16)

This is the Christian life: to be a life-giving tree, even as Jesus was. I pray the Lord woos and beckons you into a deeper intimacy as you feel the burn of His love upon your heart. There is no greater goal than to walk in His presence. Pioneers of His presence must have this solid foundation of abiding in God.

Abiding in God never graduates from the secret place life with the Lord, but it does transcend set-aside times of prayer. It is an inner reality that changes everything on the inside, and in time, the outside.

Chapter 3

GOD'S LOVE LANGUAGE

Language is the foundation of communication. If two people aren't speaking the same language, communication cannot happen effectively.

Communication is the foundation of relationship. Without it, we cannot have relationship. A relationship that is void of communication is not a relationship at all.

We know this in our earthly relationships, and the same applies to our walk with God.

I learned early in my marriage what "love languages" were. (As a matter of fact, I'm still learning how to successfully speak my wife's love language.) A love language is the way a particular person best receives love. It is the type of communication that a person best feels love from another. Our love languages vary from touch, to time, gifts, and even acts of service or words of affirmation.* We are all wired differently in how we best "hear" the language of love coming from another. I may feel most loved when receiving gifts; however, my wife may receive love more by acts of service or care. Though I may love my wife, if I don't do things for her in a way that she truly appreciates or receives love, I may

---

* Gary Chapman, *The 5 Love Languages: The Secret to Love that Lasts*, Northfield Publishing.

fail at making her feel loved. It is of the utmost importance that I understand her love languages so as to express my love to her in a way that she can receive it to the fullest. My wife loves quality time, so when I give her quality time, her "love tank" is filled.

Language is to communication what communication is to relationship.

Learning God's love language, then, is of the utmost importance to our relationship with Him.

God has made clear what He desires of us. He desires our love. He desires a heart that is in love with Him and is obedient to His word. But the former does not come without the latter being in place. A truly obedient heart will be the overflow of a heart in love. Jesus' words tell us this plainly in John 14.

> *He who has My commandments and keeps them is the one who loves Me*; and he who loves Me will be loved by My Father, and I will love him and will disclose Myself to him." Judas (not Iscariot) said to Him, "Lord, what then has happened that You are going to disclose Yourself to us and not to the world?" Jesus answered and said to him, "*If anyone loves Me, he will keep My word*; and My Father will love him, and We will come to him and make Our abode with him. *He who does not love Me does not keep My words*; and the word which you hear is not Mine, but the Father's who sent Me. (John 14:21–24, emphasis mine)

Let's read the main emphasis here in this Scripture that I have italicized.

He who has My commandments and keeps them is the one who loves Me.

If anyone loves Me, he will keep My word.
He who does not love Me does not keep My words.

If you love Jesus, you will do what He asks and commands you to do.

If you focus on loving God, you will naturally keep His word.

If you do not love God, you cannot expect to keep His words.

We are not trying to follow God's commands in order to prove our love. You can do the commands without knowing Jesus. The focus is to love Jesus, and the overflow of that is that we keep His words. Jesus makes it abundantly clear that obedience to His commands and love go hand in hand, but that is not how our religious leanings would make it seem. We must read these Scriptures as sons and daughters, not as orphans. Only then will we extract the pure nectar that lies within this word. Reading the aforementioned verses as an orphan dealing with a God who has only conditional love based on our own works causes us to receive a heavy yoke of religion upon ourselves. We then equate the power or strength of our love for God with the strength of how we feel our obedience is or how well we are "performing." This causes us to put our focus on what we are doing *for* God to prove our love rather than loving God and allowing our relationship with Him to enhance our works.

Read those Scriptures until this simple truth sinks into your heart.

Jesus knows that if He has our love He will have our service and we will keep His commands. Jesus here was affirming the first and greatest commandment, to love God with all of our heart, soul, mind, and strength (Mark 12:29–30). So how do we really love God? What is God's love language and how can we best show Him our love?

Worship.

Call it praise, adoration, thanksgiving, or anything you wish, but the truth is that God wants our love expressed through worship. As humans we are wired in our very nature to express love through art. It's been happening from the beginning.

Let's not make the mistake of thinking that God will always share our ideas of how to best receive love. Just because I receive love in a certain way, doesn't mean that showing my love to others in that same way will have the same effect. Many of us would make the mistake of making "Cain's offering" to God: assuming the Lord wants what we would want. Cain's offering isn't what God desires, but what we expect Him to desire. God has made it clear that He desires our love. Our worship and praise to Him is the highest form of daily love communication that He longs for.

While worship constitutes everything we do and who we are, a direct offering is found in the form of music. After all, in God's living room (throne room) there is nonstop singing of worship songs to Him, day and night, night and day (Revelation 4:8–9). Revelation 4 and 5 shows us that God's holy habitation is filled with non-stop worship through singing and the playing of instruments. Therefore, we can conclude that worship through the arts is one of the supreme love languages for God. David tapped into the powerful vehicle of worship to God through musical instruments, sounds, songs, and melodies. David was the worship leader who became the pastor! What I mean is that he was a worshiper before he was a leader. He was a priest before he was a king. After becoming king, he instituted nonstop worship in the nation of Israel. He declared with his words, his finances, and his life that worship is the highest point of the church's calling to love God. And the best part is that God loved it—so much so that He is rebuilding David's fallen tent today. Now, that's good news! Even now God is raising up worshipers to take the helm of great moves of God from the "Sauls." God is looking for leaders who have learned to be tender to and follow His presence.

True obedience is born of true love. God loves obedience more than sacrifice. He isn't impressed with our great offerings if they are done with little love. Our smallest sacrifices capture His heart if they are done with great love. This is why God loved Abel's sacrifice more than Cain's. Abel offered the sacrifice that was required, out of obedience. Cain offered a sacrifice from his own idea of what God would want. We must not fall into the trap of thinking that any sacrifice, great or small, will bring glory or honor to God without it being made through obedience and out of love.

God is so infatuated with the bride that He is now wooing her back to her first love, from which the fount of all life is found. It is no wonder that God is putting His breath behind a worship movement that is bent on making the identity of the church lovers of God. Lovers of God will be lovers of people.

> If someone says, "I love God," and hates his brother, he is a liar; for the one who does not love his brother whom he has seen, cannot love God whom he has not seen. (1 John 4:20)

Anyone who really loves God will love people also. This Scripture is not prodding us toward focusing on loving people in order to prove our love for God; it is showing the proper order of the commandments. This is why the first commandment is before the second. Lovers of God show their good works through the natural progression of pouring out love and care upon the world around them. You cannot truly encounter His love in a regular, daily way and not spill that love out to the world around you.

The Enemy will always try to get us to work harder in order to feel right in our relationship toward Jesus. True grace empowers us to love and worship Jesus not because we *have* to but because we *get* to.

God defends the worshippers of today as He did when He defended Mary sitting at His feet. Martha was complaining of her sister Mary's laziness because she was not "doing anything." Jesus defended Mary by saying that only one thing was necessary and that Mary had chosen the better part. This rebuke was made to the same religious Devil inside of Pharaoh when he accused Moses and the Israelites of being lazy for wanting to go into the wilderness to worship. Moses had asked for God's people to be allowed to go into the wilderness *to worship* (Exodus 7:16). Yet Pharaoh equated worship with not doing anything, as if worship were laziness. Therefore, the evil ruler increased the workload of the then-enslaved children of Israel (Exodus 5:4–9). The Pharaoh represents the devil in our lives. The enemy will always try to increase our workload—the workload of religion instead of entering into the rest of true worship. Many of God's people today are enslaved to this same evil ideology and theology. It causes us to work harder for the results we long to see. It causes us to look with disdain upon spending time in His presence in worship.

Worship does not equal laziness. True worshippers are the truest lovers. This is why the Father is looking for those who would worship Him in spirit and in truth (John 4:24). You must worship God in spirit, for He is spirit. Spiritual worship and spiritual sacrifice are described as this:

I appeal to you therefore, brothers, by the mercies of God, to present your bodies as a living sacrifice, holy and acceptable to God, which is your spiritual worship. (Romans 12:1)

You also, as living stones, are being built up as a spiritual house for a holy priesthood, to offer up spiritual sacrifices acceptable to God through Jesus Christ. (1 Peter 2:5)

Through Him then, let us continually offer up a sacrifice of praise to God, that is, the fruit of lips that give thanks to His name. (Hebrews 13:15)

God wants continual praise, presenting our entire lives as a living sacrifice. Sacrifices in the Old Testament usually had one thing in common: they were dead. God wants living sacrifices so we can be walking, mobile altars of His fire and presence!

Worshipping in truth is simply meaning what we say. Sometimes that isn't always pretty, but God will always desire the real and ugly over the fake and pretty. This is why David's psalms are a perpetual roller-coaster ride through His walk with God, up and down and up and down. This is also why God justifies the man who beats his breast in repentance and humility, not even looking to heaven; but God looks with disdain upon the super-elite religious Pharisees who make great and beautiful prayers. This is why God answered the prayer of Hannah, the mother of Samuel, whose intercessions before God were like muddled, drunken babbling. Truth in worship means that our words and worship to God are from our hearts and not our heads (or just lyrics on the projector screen at church). Jesus quoted Isaiah when he said,

"You are a people who honor God with your lips but your heart is far from Him."

God is not after lip service, but heart service. When we lay hold of a lifestyle of worship, everything changes. Worshipping God isn't a duty; it's a privilege. Our personal worship times should outnumber our corporate worship times, and the same is true of prayer. I want to fill my Father's heart. I want to reward the Lamb with my true love in worship. I want to fill His heart with the love language of worship!

God, show us Your heart and let us continually grow in the knowledge of how to express our love to You!

Chapter 4

GOD'S ORDER

It has always been God's ultimate desire to have a love-filled relationship with His creation. The entire Bible points to this, from Genesis to Revelation. God wants laborers who are consumed with their mission on earth but not without having been endued with power and love from on high.

We cannot separate the mission from the Man. How can we truly love if we don't know Love Himself? Love is not a list of dos and don'ts to check off of our list. True love supersedes all philosophy, wisdom, and knowledge because Love is a person and His name is Jesus. Can we really love without knowing Love Himself? Can we spread the character, influence, and reign of a King we don't know and submit to personally? I say it is folly to preach the gospel of a man we do not know. We cannot lead people into a relationship with another person if we ourselves don't know that person. That person is Jesus, and knowing Him is the supreme goal of our lives. Therefore, our aim is to be in love with Jesus and to make the end of all we do be for the love of God.

Even the old-covenant Jewish people knew this. Look at what the Jews call the Shema. It consists of the following Scripture in Deuteronomy:

Hear, O Israel! The Lord is our God, the Lord is one! *You shall love the LORD your God with all your heart and with all your soul and with all your might.* These words, which I am commanding you today, shall be on your heart. You shall teach them diligently to your sons and shall talk of them when you sit in your house and when you walk by the way and when you lie down and when you rise up. You shall bind them as a sign on your hand and they shall be as frontals on your forehead. You shall write them on the doorposts of your house and on your gates. (Deuteronomy 6:4–9, emphasis mine)

To ancient and modern Jews alike, this is one of the most significant portions of the Torah. It is also the most recited and beloved prayer of the Jewish people. Many recite this Scripture as a prayer every morning, every night, and at all meetings and special occasions. But because of the veil that remains upon all who have not received Christ, this ritual is practiced without much understanding.

Today, we approach this in the light of the revelation of Christ the Messiah.

It's easy to feel the pulse of God's intention in this Scripture. God is seeking wholehearted lovers of Himself. His eyes search to and fro upon the earth to find those whose heart is fully His (2 Chronicles 16:9), and the Father is seeking worshippers who worship in spirit and in truth. God is after our hearts. He desires our love. This is the one command that is above all others.

God knew, even in Old Testament times, as Jesus later testified, that all the Law and the Prophets hang on the commandment of love (Matthew 22:40). All life flows from love—loving God and loving others. God exhorted His people in ancient times to meditate on this all day, every day, when they woke, when they worked, when they rested, when they lay down to sleep, and so on, so that the end to all life would be for the love of God. In *The Practice of the Presence of God* Brother Lawrence wisely stated that God does not regard the greatness of the work we do for God, but rather the love with which a work is performed.

Before any of our gifts, knowledge, or wisdom, may we impart first and foremost the hunger to go deep in intimacy and fellowship with the Lord. If we teach our children to go only to the top of the mountains of culture to be kings of the hill, while neglecting to instruct them on how to be priests in the secret, we will reap a Christianity of dead religion and stale, institutionalized doctrines that resemble this world more than His world. I refuse any teaching that emphasizes seeking favor with man before favor with God. I question any discipleship that encourages cultural mountain climbers over God-fearing servants. In the end it isn't either-or, it's both-and. Give me a generation of priests and I'll show you a culture affected and infected with the kingdom of God.

> "Teacher, which is the great commandment in the law?" And He said to him, "'You shall love the Lord Your God with all your heart, and with all your soul, and with all your mind.' *This is the great and foremost commandment.* The second is like it, 'You shall love your neighbor as yourself.' On these two commandments depend the whole law and the prophets." (Matthew 22:36–40, emphasis mine)

The New Testament gospel accounts show that Jesus put an order to the commands. His entire discipleship process emphasized and reiterated the first commandment as an anchor and foundation of life in God. God is a God of order. But His order and our order can be two different things. God's order doesn't involve a color-coordinating sanctuary, straight rows of chairs, and church service on Sunday that begins and ends at precisely the right time. God's order doesn't mean He never makes people feel uncomfortable. In fact, He loves to break out of our boxes, and He does so without apology. If you wish to view God's magnificent order, take a walk in the forest and tell me how many straight lines you see. Though nature appears to have no order to our natural eyes, closer examination reveals that all creation is driven with incredible direction and attention to detail, more than we've even yet discovered!

When Jesus said that the first and greatest commandment is to love God with all our heart, soul, mind, and strength, He meant for us to seek this out with the most emphasis. All other commandments flow from this first and greatest one. Without this command in its proper place, we should not expect to do the works of Christ. Nor should we expect to see His kingdom come to earth in the way He desires it to.

The second commandment to love can only be truly adhered to by setting the first in place. When we love others as an overflow of our love for God, the results can match biblical proportions. <u>And when we make God our primary relational concern, all other relationships are blessed as a result</u>. Jesus made this clear when He commanded that we love Him more than our spouses, our children, our siblings, or our parents (Matthew 10:37). When we love Jesus as number one, our love for others increases exponentially. Why? Because as we come to know, experience, and live in relationship with Love Himself, we become conformed to His image. And God is love.

What's the Point

It's a slow fade into idolatry when we allow our gaze to be fixed upon serving others or even serving God, rather than simply loving Him. We have now in the western world many "seeker sensitive" churches that, mostly out of a pure heart to reach the world, have become more sensitive to the needs of man than to the unction of the Holy Spirit. The last few decades, following the great evangelical thrust of the '40s and '50s with men of God like Billy Graham, have set our main goals as saving souls. This was the hand of the Lord, restoring a measure of mass evangelism to the church and seeing a multitude of people come into the kingdom. We should honor these moves of God and the men who were used mightily in them. And we should build upon them. However, lacking the foundation of the prophets and apostles, we gradually began to believe that once we saved souls, we were to simply hold on for heaven until we died instead of taking dominion in the earth. Much of our main goal in the church today is to simply see more people saved.

I agree that the most powerful miracle on earth is the salvation of someone's eternal soul. And the gospel of salvation is needed. But the gospel of the kingdom teaches us how to grow up into the fullness of Christ. Our conviction to see people saved has put a yoke of heaviness around the bride and caused us to settle for only a piece of the good news. It has caused us to put the second commandment, to love people, above the first, to love God.

When saving souls becomes more important than loving God, we "cheat" God's order. We cannot save anyone. Only Jesus Christ can. Of course He uses us to do this. But while God throws a party every time one sinner returns to Him, it is our love and worship that He is ultimately after. How sad that our churches are full of people who've been saved from hell but who aren't living to give God their hearts in worship! How pathetic would it be to see the whole world evangelized only to forget about God in the busyness of our work for Him! When love for God is cultivated in our lives, we will naturally be the love of Jesus at all times to everyone we meet.

I believe that instead of trying to get conversions, we should seek to love people, regardless of any other motive than love itself. Love will make disciples, and that's what we're after!

This mixing of the order of divine priority is how we end up with churches full of orphans instead of sons and daughters. Orphans work to constantly be loved because they believe they have to do good things and attain success to be loved. Sons and daughters of God do good works *because of love, not for it*. Those who bring people into the kingdom, and into a culture of "second commandment over the first," create orphans who are not truly discipled or fathered. We save people and then tell them their job is now to save more people. If we are only concerned with saving souls and getting decisions for Christ, we put another tally on our belt and move on. And these orphans find credibility and love from doing more and more works.

Jesus didn't call us to get people saved but to disciple them and preach the gospel of the kingdom of God. Oh for a generation that would find success in being at the feet of Jesus, being loved and loving Him!

You can only bear fruit with these disordered commandments for so long until you become dry and unusable. Jesus made it clear that if we didn't abide in Him we could not bear fruit. If you don't abide, prepare to be dry. To abide in God's presence and be fruitful is the foundational essence of the kingdom mandate, from Genesis to Revelation. But if the second commandment is your root, "seeker sensitive" will be your fruit.

The seeker-sensitive movement is not wrong in its pursuit of relevance. But to not allow the Holy Spirit to have His way in His own meetings with His people is arrogance. Seeking to please people before pleasing God is out of order. God wants us to serve others, but if we focus on the things of man before the things of God, we are operating in the demonic.

Jesus states this plainly in Matthew 16:23. After Peter rebuked Him and said he wouldn't allow Jesus to go to the cross, Jesus said, "Get behind me, Satan, for you have in mind the things of man and not the things of God." Peter thought he was doing the right thing, like many leaders in the church today who are trying to meet the people's needs. Yet his mind was in agreement with satan in that he was focused first and foremost on the things of man, not of God. God's ways are different from ours. We must pursue His ways and be in agreement with what He is doing, even if it seems contrary to our thoughts or plans. If our relationship with the Lord is strong, and kept current each and every day, we will have the resolve to stand before all people to do what He has told us to do. We want to make God comfortable in our meetings, and we want Him to rest in our midst. If God is there, people will gather on dirt floors and in barns to connect with Him!

God desires our attention. Worshipping Him is the simple act of turning our eyes upon Him. Most of the time the Enemy does not try to get our eyes on him, but to get us to worship anything other than God alone. This is the great worship war of all history. Romans 1:25 speaks to this:

> They exchanged the truth of God for a lie, and *worshiped and served the creature rather than the Creator*, who is blessed forever. Amen.

This Scripture speaks of the ungodly, not necessarily believers. But many Christians today exchange the truth for a lie when they worship and serve the creature rather than the Creator.

If we switch the first and second commandments, not giving them their proper order in our personal life and in the corporate life of the church, we will reap ungodliness and be ineffective in bringing the kingdom of God to earth in the way it was meant to be. The most profound ministries on earth will come from those who have Jesus Christ as their supreme love.

We are all prone to drifting from this. If we do not proactively seek after the first commandment, we are in danger of shifting our perspectives away from what really matters. In the end we will stand before God Almighty, not man. Not loving God and being in intimate relationship with Him is unacceptable. He is raising up a bride that is without spot or wrinkle, clothed in the purity of a heart that gazes upon Jesus.

Pioneers across the earth are now humbly and boldly proclaiming that we need to return to God with a heart of pure worship. Worship is not the warm-up to the main event; it *is* the main event. All teaching and preaching should inspire more wholehearted love for Jesus.

Won't you pray the following prayer with me?

God, restore the first commandment in my life in all I do. Holy Spirit, prioritize my agendas in life. I want You to get the firstfruits, and I desire that the foundation of all I do would be born from the place of being a wholehearted, wild lover of You. Let the love I have for You be spilled out into the world around me.

Chapter 5

GOOD WORKERS ARE GOOD LOVERS

The best workers will be the best lovers. Workers work until the day is done. They watch the clock for the end of the day to come. They stop when the day is done and they expect to get paid extra if they work overtime.

Lovers can't keep track of time. The clock is irrelevant, as they enjoy what they are doing. After all, time flies when you're having fun! No one has to tell two lovers to talk to each other. They can't stay apart! When you are doing something you love, you work from the place of joy.

God is looking for lovers. Those who would advance His kingdom on earth because of their great love for Him and their desire to see Him glorified. Lovers will lay down their lives day after day, and they do it cheerfully. God isn't looking for people who drudgingly go through the laborious works of the kingdom. He is after those who cheerfully give. God loves a cheerful giver, not a complaining one!

Lovers are almost unaware of the good works they have done. When courting my wife before marriage, I talked to her for hours at a time. No one had to remind me to talk to her, buy her flowers, or do nice things for her. It happened naturally because she was always on my mind. She still is today! This is what the Lord has called us to do: to abide in Him throughout our days.

Let's read this amazing example in Scripture.

> When the Son of Man comes in His glory, and all the holy angels with Him, then He will sit on the throne of His glory. All the nations will be gathered before Him, and He will separate them one from another, as a shepherd divides his sheep from the goats. And He will set the sheep on His right hand, but the goats on the left.
>
> Then the King will say to those on His right hand, "Come, you blessed of My Father, inherit the kingdom prepared for you from the foundation of the world: for I was hungry and you gave Me food; I was thirsty and you gave Me drink; I was a stranger and you took Me in; I was naked and you clothed Me; I was sick and you visited Me; I was in prison and you came to Me."
>
> Then the righteous will answer Him, saying, "Lord, when did we see You hungry and feed You, or thirsty and give You drink? When did we see You a stranger and take You in, or naked and clothe You? Or when did we see You sick, or in prison, and come to You?"
>
> And the King will answer and say to them, "Assuredly, I say to you, inasmuch as you did it to one of the least of these My brethren, you did it to Me." (Matthew 25:31–40 NKJV)

This is a prophetic foretelling of how Christ will judge people at the end of the age. Reread that Scripture passage and notice how the righteous believers responded to Jesus:

> "When did we do all these good things?"

<u>These believers are clueless to all the good they have done</u>. They live in such a way that the overflow of their lives touches the world around them and also the heart of Jesus. They are an example of how loving and knowing God becomes the source of good works.

Their ignorance of their good works is in direct correlation to Matthew 6, where Jesus tells us to do our spiritual activities in secret so that we may reap a reward with God and not with men. The righteous ones that Jesus speaks to here in Matthew 25 have tapped into this relationship. They have no idea that they had done these good works unto the Lord.

This is how we are to be as well. But it's not easy.

When I do something sacrificial for another person, I find it difficult to keep that between just the Lord and me. The first thing I want to do is tell my wife or friends about my selfless act. But in Matthew 6, Jesus said th<u>at when we do something for others we are to keep it between Him and us</u>, because if we boast about it before people, we will lose our reward with God.

How is it then that these people at the very end will not even be aware of their good and righteous acts? I believe the answer is that their good works flowed from their good love. Time and time again in my walk with Christ, I have seen that it is the small, seemingly insignificant things that end up having the greatest impact. <u>When I simply live to love God, I end up loving people more effectively</u>.

The lovers will always out-work the workers. Lovers do good deeds because they *get to*; workers do them because they *have to*. Lovers will go the extra mile, while workers will ask for overtime pay. Workers do a job to get it done; lovers do a task with their hearts behind it.

Jesus wants lovers, not workers. The most zealous religious workers will not fill the heart of God or change the world. Only through the simplicity of knowing Love Himself and letting His love overflow in us will we do what needs to be done in advancing the kingdom of God on earth. This is why I'm burning to build and cultivate cultures of loving God first and foremost in the church.

Does your heart not burn to know Him? Then put worship and prayer at the center of your lifestyle. From this place, the greatest works the world has ever seen will be accomplished!

To Know Him

In marriage, after the honeymoon is over and a few years have gone by, you need to make time for each other. Not just to get stuff done, but to engage each other in intimacy. The same is true in our relationship with God. The supreme priority of their lives must be to know and love Jesus.

The worship and prayer surge in the church today is calling us back, individually and corporately, to this first love. God is jealous for His church to truly know Him. I have seen this all over the world. Never before has such a global movement in the church occurred, where people are hungry to know God in an intimate and personal way.

> "He made known His ways to Moses, His acts to the sons of Israel." (Psalm 103:7)

Do not be deceived—God's ways and His acts are two different things. Moses knew God's ways; He knew God face-to-face and was a close friend of the Lord. The people of God in Moses' day knew of God's acts and witnessed many incredible things, but they did not know God in an intimate way. Jesus came to earth for this very purpose. And through relationship with God, His people can destroy the works of darkness and advance His kingdom.

The Scriptures make it terrifyingly clear that many different types of people will stand before God in the judgment. Even more admonishing, many who think they are Christians because of their works will follow the path to hell.

> Not everyone who says to Me, "Lord, Lord," will enter the kingdom of heaven, but he who does the will of My Father who is in heaven will enter. Many will say to Me on that day, "Lord, Lord, did we not prophesy in Your name, and in Your name cast out demons, and in Your name perform many miracles?" And then I will declare to them, "I never knew you; depart from Me, you who practice lawlessness." (Matthew 7:21–23)

These people will stand before Jesus, calling Him Lord as if to persuade Him of their worthiness. Then they will give a list of everything they did for God in their lifetime, believing that relationship can be founded upon good works and accomplished quotas. But Jesus will look upon them and say, "I never knew you."

How terrifying it would be to be surprised with this chilling statement.

If you have to read your resume to someone in order to prove that you know that individual, odds are you are fighting a losing battle. Imagine going to a celebrity's private party, and when you try to gain entrance, you list all the things you've done for him and how much you've read about him. Those things don't hold weight in real relationships.

A list of accomplishments may be a good way to enter into a business relationship, because business is formal. But family is intimately personal. And God wants a family, not a well-run business.

If we constantly put our time and energy into doing works for God, we are right on track to being in this group that cries, "Lord, Lord" at the judgment.

Note that Jesus didn't commend the righteous in Matthew 25 on the things that man considers "big," like casting out demons, healing the sick, or prophesying. Rather, His heart was impressed and moved with how they performed simple acts of kindness and love: a glass of water, visiting the down and out, caring for the lowly and the least of these.

True lovers of God will do the true acts of God. If we think we are serving God based on our work schedule for Him, we have missed the point. God wants us so wrapped up in this love relationship that we lose our lives, even the thought of doing "good" or "bad." Eating from the tree of the knowledge of good and evil produced death for Adam and Eve, and it still does for us today. Only by eating of the intimacy that comes from relationship with Jesus can we truly live and be life to others.

The church is called to truly know Christ. Not as a means to assurance of salvation. But for a life rooted in a love relationship with God. Good works will flow from good lovers.

Chapter 6

THE MASTER

God is restoring proper order to His church. Throughout Jesus' ministry we see Him pulling His disciples back to the place of loving and serving Him alone, putting Him first.

It pays to look at the way the "greats" in any field do what they do. If a person is successful in business, we mimic certain techniques he or she uses. If someone excels in athletics, we study his or her workout routines. Wisdom in life issues is also best gained from people who have been through similar things and succeeded.

When it comes to discipleship, Jesus is the textbook example. He took eleven ordinary men, made them His disciples, and flipped the world and all of history upside down. These few men bore fruit that is around even today. That is fruit that lasts.

Discipleship is foundational and vital to the kingdom. It embodies the very essence of the kingdom mandate. God gave this mandate in the garden to Adam and Eve when He told them to take dominion in the earth, and to be fruitful and multiply (Genesis 1:28). Jesus restored humanity to God through the cross and His resurrection, and He gave the same mandate to all who believe through the Great Commission (Matthew 28:18–20). This commissioning is one of taking dominion in the earth by way of being fruitful and multiplying. It is heaven coming to earth, His will being done here on earth as it is in heaven.

Whether naturally or spiritually, there is no surer way to multiply than to reproduce yourself in others. As Christians, we are to reproduce others who follow Christ as we do.

Think of it! The Lord of all creation has entrusted to us the responsibility of making disciples. That shows the enormous faith Christ has in us.

Jesus gave us clear commands to follow. He even shortened the list from ten down to two. Love God *first*, and love people *second*.

Now, don't confuse commands with assignments. A command is something we prioritize or draw attention to. An assignment is a specific task or work we see to accomplish. Our priority must be to love God and love people. Our assignment flows out of this. It's important not to run after an "assignment" in ministry while neglecting the priority of being a lover of Jesus. Only by knowing Love Himself can we give love to a broken world. Our love assignment flows from our love relationship with Him. And we must use this model while making disciples of Jesus. The apostle Paul told the believers at Corinth to not stray away from the simplicity of pure devotion to Christ (2 Corinthians 11:2–3).

Jesus lived, traveled, taught, and did ministry with His disciples. There was no "new believers class" one hour a week for three months. This was intentional and deliberate community. And while our western culture seems unsuitable for this type of discipleship, I believe it challenges our modern ideas of how to multiply mature believers and bring forth true increase.

This underlying theme of intimacy invades the rest of the discipleship process. To know Him, we need to learn His character, His ways, His personality—to simply be with Him!

Jesus continually turned the disciples' hearts toward loving

God first. Throughout the gospel accounts of Jesus' ministry, we see this priority of keeping the first and great commandment at the forefront of their focus.

One of the clearest pictures of this is the classic story found in Luke 10.

> As Jesus and his disciples were on their way, he came to a village where a woman named Martha opened her home to him. She had a sister called Mary, who sat at the Lord's feet listening to what he said. But Martha was distracted by all the preparations that had to be made. She came to him and asked, "Lord, don't you care that my sister has left me to do the work by myself? Tell her to help me!"
>
> "Martha, Martha," the Lord answered, "you are worried and upset about many things, but few things are needed—or indeed only one. Mary has chosen what is better, and it will not be taken away from her." (Luke 10:38–42)

Martha represents the worker who is serving Jesus, Mary the lover who is sitting at His feet, listening and meditating on His word. Many teach that we as the body of Christ need to have those who work *and* those who pray. This is what insecure workers use to justify their striving, to feel like they are in good standing with God. I know this because I have been that person! However, Jesus forever settled the question when He justified Mary and said that she had chosen the one necessary thing, the better part, and it would not be taken from her.

He echoed King David's heart in Psalm 27:4:

> *One thing* I have asked from the Lord, that I shall seek: that I may dwell in the house of the LORD all the days of

my life, to behold the beauty of the LORD and to meditate in His temple. (Psalm 27:4, emphasis mine)

> Jesus wants our love, affection, and attention more than our service or "good works." The times we don't live out of this truth will be the times when we feel most insecure, lost, and confused.

First-Love Discipleship

I want to share a few stories of how Jesus emphasized first love within the discipleship process of His immediate followers.

The first comes from a look at the life of Simon Peter. Peter's life, at least what we see in the gospel accounts prior to the resurrection of Christ, characterizes the believer who is full of zeal for Christ, even willing to die for the cause of Christ. This type of believer is pure in heart, but mistakenly misplaces the strength of his relationship with Jesus on his own zeal rather than in Jesus' love. This pitfall is a common one. Even more common is the lie that we must serve and even fight for God, because this is how we show God we love Him. While it's true that serving and loving others is a good thing to do, it must be an overflow of our love for the Father. This is clearly seen in the Martha and Mary scenario.

> From that time Jesus began to show His disciples that He must go to Jerusalem, and suffer many things from the elders and chief priests and scribes, and be killed, and be raised up on the third day. Peter took Him aside and began to rebuke Him, saying, "God forbid it, Lord! This shall never happen to You." But He turned and said to Peter, "Get behind Me, Satan! You are a stumbling block to Me; for you are not setting your mind on God's interests, but man's." (Matthew 16:21–23)

Peter was sitting among the believers when Jesus spoke about how He was soon to be crucified, and we see His zeal come forth. Peter actually rebuked God! Oh that our zeal would not cause us to rebuke the Lord for His plans and His ways!

At the Last Supper, Jesus spoke again of how all of His followers would abandon Him and fall away that very night. Peter was the first to jump to his own defense, saying in essence, "All of the other disciples may deny You, but I never will. I will lay down my life for You even now!"

How many people have you heard say, "I will go anywhere and do anything for Jesus; I would even become a martyr for the sake of the gospel"? This passion isn't bad, and people who say such things do not have impure hearts. But zeal must be ultimately rooted in our love relationship with God.

Jesus answered Peter with a quiet reply. "Truly I say to you, before the morning comes and rooster crows you will deny me three times." (Mark 14:30)

When this very thing happened, the foundation of Peter's faith was revealed to be lacking. His relationship with Jesus wasn't lacking in passion. It wasn't even lacking sacrificially. Peter left everything to follow Jesus. But Peter's walk with Jesus was founded in his own zeal, not in his love for Christ.

Jesus allowed this testing over Peter to do two important things.

1. So that Jesus could show His unconditional and unfailing love to Peter in that He would take him back with no strings attached, even after Peter deserted Him in the most trying part of His life. The love of Jesus for us is the fuel for our passion and zeal.

2. So that Peter would learn to base his entire life, and especially his future ministry, on one thing: love. Our fire for God comes from His love, remembering that He loved us first. Jesus

wanted to make sure Peter would live with the supreme goal of loving Him before serving Him. Obedience is greater than sacrifice (1 Samuel 15:22), and true obedience comes from true love, not the other way around.

After the resurrection of Christ, Peter went back to his old occupation of fishing. He saw Jesus on the beach and they reunited with joy. Jesus called Peter to repentance by asking three times, "Do you love me?" Each time Peter replied, "Yes, you know that I love You." Each time, Jesus said, "Then feed my sheep," or, "Then tend my lambs."

Jesus didn't make Peter publicly denounce his betrayal, nor did he make Peter feel bad for what he had done. Peter knew his error—he had wept bitterly after his betrayal, and deep repentance surely took place in his heart. Jesus received Peter back into fellowship, yet led him into a new understanding for ministry.

Notice the sequence Jesus established with Peter. He asked, "Do you love me?" Then He told him, "Feed my sheep." Jesus asked again, "Do you love me?" Then He told him, "Tend to my lambs." Our ministry to others must come from the place of loving God first. If loving Jesus is your first priority, let that love overflow into ministry.

Jesus solidified Peter's life in the first and great commandment. The zealous Peter denied Jesus to a little girl, but the Peter rooted in love went to an upside-down cross to be martyred for His name.

To love God is first priority, and all our work for the Lord must be anchored from that place. Otherwise, our work becomes boastful and we become zealous for serving to the point where we are rebuking God's plans and working for God in order to establish our own righteousness and worth. The good news is that we get to delve into the depths of God's unending love, and as we discover this love we respond in love, creating vibrant relationship.

This overflow touches the world around us and brings His kingdom and all of its resources to earth!

Offensive Love

As the disciples walked with the God-Man, learning His ways, they also did the works that He did. Yet Jesus always pulled their hearts back to worshipping Him.

Matthew 25 shows a scene from judgment day when Jesus commends the righteous for works they were unaware of. These works include giving glasses of water to the thirsty, visiting prisoners, clothing the naked, and other simple acts of love done to the least of all people.

Right after that teaching, Jesus went to Bethany, and Mary came into the house Jesus was at and poured an extremely expensive jar of perfume all over Him.

> While Jesus was in Bethany in the home of Simon the Leper, a woman came to him with an alabaster jar of very expensive perfume, which she poured on his head as he was reclining at the table.
>
> When the disciples saw this, they were indignant. "Why this waste?" they asked. "This perfume could have been sold at a high price and the money given to the poor."
>
> Aware of this, Jesus said to them, "Why are you bothering this woman? She has done a beautiful thing to me. The poor you will always have with you, but you will not always have me. When she poured this perfume on my body, she did it to prepare me for burial. Truly I tell you, wherever this gospel is preached throughout the world, what she has done will also be told, in memory of her." (Matthew 26:6–13)

This happened after Jesus gave the disciples the prophetic account of what they would be commended for on judgment day. With this fresh on their hearts, they would be *looking* for "the least of these" on their way to Bethany, trying to live out this thing and hoping Jesus noticed!

When Mary broke the jar of perfume and poured it on Jesus, the disciples of Jesus, those who were closest to Him, became indignant. They said, "This should not have been done it could have been used to feed the poor." Fresh off of the teaching of Jesus, they responded with "She shouldn't have wasted that! It should have been used to help the least of these!"

Jesus defended Mary's exuberant act of worship by justifying her sacrifice. He even went a step further, saying that wherever the gospel was preached in all the earth, her action would be spoken of in memory of her. Wow! He essentially said that good works are great, and the poor you will always have, but worshipping Him and loving Him first is the foundation of all good works.

Feeding the poor does please God. Yet the eternal Scriptures retain this act of worship, and Jesus said it would be remembered along with the gospel. Why? Because this is the essence of the good news of the kingdom. It truly is about worship—bringing creation out of slavery to the fall and sin, and into relationship and lifestyles of worship unto God.

Worship, in any form, is the ultimate manifestation of love. Yet the religious mind finds true love offensive.

When David danced before the presence of God, his wife, Michal, looked upon him with the same disgust that the disciples showed to Mary when she poured perfume on Jesus (2 Samuel 6).

Michal was physically barren after this. It is true still today that those who find fault and criticize cannot birth the things of God.

THE MASTER

Martha equated her sister's actions of sitting at the feet of Jesus, gazing upon Him and listening to His word, as laziness. The Pharaoh of Egypt accused Moses of the same thing when Moses asked him to let God's people go so they could worship God.

All acts of extravagant worship and radical devotion will appear to many as a waste of time, talent, and money. But to the heart aflame with love, all things are considered loss compared to knowing Him more.

Loving God as our first priority is not a suggestion. It is God's wise command. If we engage God enough to discover the endless depth of His love for us, we will respond with love for Him. We love Him because we realize that He loved us first.

This love overflows into all of our earthly relationships and even into our daily, mundane activities. God wants every part of us. Let us be a people who abide in God and His awesome love, and let that love be our master. Let us be slaves to Love's leading and pour out the presence and goodness of God every minute of every day!

All of the heroes in the faith, in the Bible and throughout church history, have one common denominator: they were all lovers of God whose deepest desire was to know Him. They hungered for intimate relationship with Him. Every person who did the exploits of the kingdom on earth knew God intimately and personally. They labored in the art of the secret life with God.

Are we so foolishly bold as to try to accomplish amazing feats by the power of God while denying the power of consecration and holiness?

Part Two
The Map

Chapter 7

UNIQUE AND PROVOKING PRESENCE

I love reading in the Word about the lovers and friends of God. It excites my spirit like almost nothing else. It's as if their lives sing throughout the halls of history, provoking lame hearts to come alive and calling a generation back home to the depths of God. I love the mystery of Enoch, who walked with God so closely that God took him without letting him taste death. And Moses, who spoke with God face-to-face as a friend speaks with a friend.

I also love reading about the heroes of church history, like the Moravians, the reformers of the first and second great awakenings of the church, and modern revivalists. These men and women of God performed exploits in their generations and shaped history because of one simple yet profound thing. They loved God. They were in love with Jesus. Their love for Him and their obedience to follow Him wherever He took them *provokes* us to do the same and even more.

God wants our hearts, our love. The heart is the most valuable piece of property in the universe. Jesus deserves ours, and He is worthy of it, not only because of who He is but also because of what He has done and is still doing. And the more we surrender our hearts to the Lord, the greater He will be in our lives. The more of your heart he owns, the more of it becomes His home and His throne.

God wants His presence to be fully upon you. We should be jealous after His presence! Remember, the Hebrew and Greek definitions of God's presence in the Bible is simply "face." This manifest closeness is obtained through intimacy and friendship with Him.

We must be a people who individually and corporately know our desperate need of the presence of God. If we don't understand the necessity of His presence in and among our everyday lives, we won't desire it. If we don't desire the presence of the Lord, we won't honor it. If we don't honor His presence, we won't follow, yield, or submit to it. This will lead to a never-ending wilderness and unfruitful lives. God's ultimate goal is to bring His presence to earth by way of *us*. We are to be a nation of priests who carry with us the presence and glory of God in all of its beauty and resource.

When the children of Israel wandered in the wilderness after the exodus, God's presence was among the entire nation, but it rested upon only one man. Moses was the only one willing to go to the top of mountain. He was the only one who wanted to see God's face. In this lies a key to walking in the presence of God. Psalm 103:7 describes this plainly.

> He made known His ways to Moses, His acts to the children of Israel. (Psalm 103:7)

Moses was not satisfied in seeing only the acts of God or the moving of His hand; He wanted something deeper than the rest of the nation of Israel. His desire was to know Him, to know His ways.

In the church today, we enjoy the moving of His hand, yet often fail to seek His face. Like the children of Israel, we want the crossing of the Red Sea but we refuse to go up to the mountain to meet with God. We love manna from heaven but we dare not enter into the tent of meeting.

We come to our meetings and conferences longing to encounter the moving of His hand. But once the meeting ends, we aren't too interested in seeking His face. I've seen people roll on the floor in revival meetings, but not hunger and thirst for Him the morning after, when no one is watching. We think that working for God is the same as knowing Him. The church in America is satisfied with worshipping God through singing words on a screen in the sanctuary, yet rarely prays to the Lord in private.

I'm not saying that God's hand moving is bad. On the contrary! It is right and good for us to love miracles, signs and wonders, and all other movings of God among us. But let us not be satisfied with the hand of God and forsake the seeking of His face. The seeking of His face will always lead to the moving of His hand.

I know this personally and have seen firsthand how it happens. I have seen how we will flock to the special speaker and the guest leader, but the prayer closet is empty the next morning and the prayer room is empty that following week. Let us not be like the nine lepers that Jesus healed who didn't return to thank Him, and then to follow Him. Let us be like the one who returned to know Him and was made completely whole (Luke 17:11–19).

The acts of God are meant to provoke us to know Him personally. Miracles of healing showcase God's love in order that we may love Him back. God moves in our midst to provoke a response. Real relationship results in service as we show love for one another. And God is after wholehearted lovers.

Although God chose Moses to be the leader of Israel, He

desired more that Moses would seek His face. God's chosen successor for Moses was one of the few people in the nation who sought God's presence as much as Moses. Joshua led God's people into the greater promises God had given. His proving grounds for His right to be the next leader were found on his face outside the tent of meeting. He lingered outside of Moses' tent long after Moses left meeting with God (Exodus 33:11). In fact, Joshua received instructions on how to take the city of Jericho during a time of worship (Joshua 5:15).

The leaders of tomorrow are those who seek intimacy with God today.

> Moses used to take the tent and pitch it outside the camp, a good distance from the camp, and he called it the tent of meeting. And everyone who sought the LORD would go out to the tent of meeting that was outside the camp. And it came about, whenever Moses went out to the tent that all the people would arise and stand, each at the entrance of his tent, and gaze after Moses until he entered the tent. Whenever Moses entered the tent, the pillar of cloud would descend and stand at the entrance of the tent; and the LORD would speak with Moses. When all the people saw the pillar of cloud standing at the entrance of the tent, all the people would arise and worship, each at the entrance of his tent. Thus the LORD used to speak to Moses face to face, just as a man speaks to his friend. When Moses returned to the camp, his servant Joshua, the son of Nun, a young man, would not depart from the tent. (Exodus 33:7–11)

Moses knew that the presence of God was the defining factor of a people. His prayers reveal His priority to the presence of God.

UNIQUE AND PROVOKING PRESENCE

Then Moses said to the LORD, "See, You say to me, 'Bring up this people!' But You Yourself have not let me know whom You will send with me. Moreover, You have said, 'I have known you by name, and you have also found favor in My sight.' Now therefore, I pray You, if I have found favor in Your sight, let me know Your ways that I may know You, so that I may find favor in Your sight. Consider too, that this nation is Your people."

And He said, "My presence shall go *with you*, and I will give you rest."

Then he said to Him, "If Your presence does not go *with us*, do not lead us up from here. For how then can it be known that I have found favor in Your sight, I and Your people? Is it not by Your going with us, so that we, I and Your people, may be *distinguished* from all the other people who are upon the face of the earth?" (Exodus 33:12–16 emphasis mine)

Moses interceded for God's presence to go with them. Earlier, as recorded in Exodus 33, God told Moses that He would take them to the Promised Land but that His presence would not go with them. What a terrifying thought! It is possible to get to all of our promises and not have the presence of God when we get there.

If our prophetic promises from God become more precious to us than His presence, we will have missed the point. God is so faithful that He will give us what He promised, but His presence will not be in our midst.

Through Moses' prayer we get a foundational truth. He says, "Is it not by Your presence upon Your people that distinguishes us from all the other people upon the earth?" What makes us different in the earth as sons and daughters of God is not our bumper stickers, Christian slogans, or social media posts; it is the presence of God upon us. Without it, we don't stand out from the world. We can't be salt and light to the earth if we don't have His presence. The greatest call of the Christian in these days is to walk with God in intimacy. Our call is to carry His presence upon ourselves like priests and then to release it in the earth as kings.

The presence of God stirs up and arouses zeal in us. Anytime we encounter another person who carries the authority of His presence, we should be provoked to know God in the same way. We are called to provoke others to know Him as we carry His presence, or His face, upon us.

When we carry His presence, the image of who He is, we can introduce others to Him. People don't need an impersonal God or fine-sounding arguments of why they should follow God. But when they see Him face-to-face as we carry His presence, they will be aroused in the very makeup of who they are to know the God who created them and loves them. God is rebuilding a place for His presence all across the earth so that men can seek His face. David's tabernacle was also rebuilt for this same reason.

> After this I will return and rebuild David's fallen tent. Its ruins I will rebuild, and I will restore it, that the rest of mankind may seek the Lord, even all the Gentiles who bear my name. (Acts 15:16–17)

We are to wear a provoking presence of the Lord upon us. We are to stir up others to know God like we know Him, even within the household of faith.

Paul mentions provoking His countrymen to jealousy through the blessing of God upon the new covenant believer: "…

UNIQUE AND PROVOKING PRESENCE

if somehow I could provoke my people to jealousy and save some of them" (Romans 11:4).

We want to provoke others to godly jealousy, that they would hunger after God because of what they see upon us. Godly jealousy is being selfish for someone for unselfish reasons. It's being zealous for someone's overall well-being with selfless motives.

Paul said that he wanted to provoke jealousy in his own people so that some of them might be saved. Isn't that the outcome we are looking for? That the people in our cities and nations would come to know Jesus Christ, the Son of God, as their personal Savior and walk as a follower of Him. Paul wanted to see the nation of Israel and Jews everywhere come to Christ. We too can provoke people to know their Messiah as we carry His provoking presence.

David wanted to bring the ark (God's presence in the Old Testament) back to Jerusalem. His journey was not an easy one. He had tried the first time and Uzzah was struck down for trying to steady the ark as it was being carried on a cart. Read what happened next.

> David was afraid of the Lord that day; he said, "How can the ark of the Lord come into my care?" So David was unwilling to take the ark of the Lord into his care in the city of David; instead David took it to the house of Obed-Edom the Gittite. The ark of the Lord remained in the house of Obed-Edom the Gittite for three months; and the Lord blessed Obed-Edom and all his household. It was told King David, "The Lord has blessed the household of Obed-Edom and all that belongs to him, because of the ark of God." So David went and brought up the ark of God from the house of Obed-Edom to the city of David with rejoicing. (2 Samuel 6:9–12)

Obed-Edom wasn't a Jew. He was a foreigner who had converted to the faith. Because he was a faithful follower of Jehovah, David trusted the ark to him.

Obed-Edom was a Gentile, grafted into the family of God just like those of us who have come to Christ through faith.

When King David was told how much Obed-Edom's household was blessed, the news provoked Him to go after the presence himself. It stirred David up to finish what he had started. A Gentile provoked a Jew because he hosted the presence of God.

This is what we are called to do today. We are to provoke all the nations of the earth, not only the Jews, by carrying the presence of God. The desire for Christ is in the hearts of all people, knowingly or not. We draw that desire out when we carry the presence of God.

Though many people can see the beauty of nature, they do not all come to know Christ. There is a difference between God's omnipresence and His manifest presence.

The presence of God is in every believer. However, in order to carry the presence of God to others, we must walk before Him in such a way that attracts people to His presence. If we guard our hearts unto Him and walk in the fear of the Lord, He will draw out this provoking presence upon us.

> Thus says the LORD, "Heaven is My throne and the earth is My footstool. Where then is a house you could build for Me? And where is a place that I may rest? For My hand made all these things, Thus all these things came into being," declares the LORD. "But to this one I will look, to him who is humble and contrite of spirit, and who trembles at My word." (Isaiah 66:1-2)

How do we attract the "look" of God as spoken here? Who does God look toward to put His Spirit upon? The one who is humble and poor in spirit and who has instant obedience in his heart to the word of God.

God says in the above Scripture that He has built and made everything, so what could we possibly do to make a place for Him? He answers His own question by declaring that there is something that we can build for Him: a lifestyle of humility, being poor in spirit and the fear of the Lord.

I charge you to hunger after God and to settle in your heart today to do what He says, no matter the cost. There is an ancient Greek proverb by a man named Seneca the Younger, which says, "It is not the man who has too little, but the man who craves more, that is poor".

We are not poor in spirit because we are content with what we have; we are poor because we always crave more. In the kingdom, craving more of God is a good and honorable thing. The degree we do so will be the degree that He can find rest in and upon our lives.

> "Blessed are the poor in spirit, for theirs is the kingdom of heaven" (Matthew 5:3).

We must put on Christ and wear His provoking presence so that others may come to know Him and so those who are of the faith will yearn to know Him even more. How do we put on Christ? Simply be with Him! Ask for the presence of God to clothe you daily and seek Him every day and in every way. Then you will not merely know of Him, but you will truly know Him intimately, and He will reside upon you!

Chapter 8

BARREN LANDS AND RIVERS IN THE DESERT

The boy Samuel ministered to the Lord before Eli. And the word of the Lord was rare in those days; there was no widespread revelation. (1 Samuel 3:1)

In the time before the prophet Samuel was born, the Bible says that the word of the Lord was rare and there was no widespread revelation. An entire nation, a whole people group, stood in the darkness of not hearing God's voice or experiencing Him in a daily way.

Hannah, Samuel's mother, longed to have a child. Her desire was more than a motherly burden to have children; the very heart of God in her spurred on intercession for a child. Hannah's petitions were not the elegant prayers of a polished preacher, but the groanings of God within her. You see, God wanted to birth from Hannah not only a prophet but an entire prophetic movement, which would culminate in the tabernacle of David.

Hannah's words of intercession were unintelligible to Eli the priest, who accused Hannah of being drunk in the temple of the Lord. She let him know that she wasn't drunk with earthly wine, but with the burden of the Lord to have a child.

Many times God uses those who are barren to give birth to the greatest gifts. He loves to show His glory through the least likely people and places so that He may confound the wisdom of the wise.

Through much intercession, Samuel was brought forth. The prophets of our day must be born the same way. There is no other option. Prophets who are "flavors of the month" may come without much prayer, but prophets who lead entire prophetic movements and change the paradigm of nations and of history must come through the intercessions of submitted vessels who welcome the Lord's burden.

Samuel was called as a Nazarite. He was to be consecrated and set apart for the work of God. Where others could, he could not. His life was one that was set apart for a special assignment. He was a type of John the Baptist. He moved in great power and authority, but his main purpose was to prepare the way for the greater things of God to come in his generation.

It will always take a prophetic, consecrated voice to make way for the fullness of God's plans to come forth. We must have Samuels to anoint the Davids, Elijahs to find the Elishas, and John the Baptists to make way for Jesus.

Samuel raised up other prophets and even prophetic musicians. From having no word of the Lord or widespread revelation in the land to having every plowboy and his brother playing instruments unto God, Samuel changed the "normal" of his day. As a young man, an unknown kid named David played the harp in the back country and sang prophetic songs.

Heavens Sounds, God's Songs

David worshipped God in the fields for years. He had learned to cultivate the presence of God in his life through praise and singing songs to the Lord. David learned early on that when he played and sang unto the Lord, even with no one around, God's presence came near to him.

After years of ministering to God in secret, David became forever linked with the prophet Samuel when Samuel came to anoint David to be the next king of Israel. From that day forward David lived not only as a priest who ministered unto God, but as a prophet who was used as a mouthpiece of Jehovah. Many of David's psalms carry the same prophetic weight of any of the Old Testament prophets.

David's first "gig" that we know about was playing for King Saul to drive away Saul's tormenting devils. To play for the king of the nation is a big break for any musician! But it was common knowledge in that day that anointed music drove demons away and brought peace and the presence of God. Scripture doesn't say that David ministered in song, only that he played melody on his harp. But the melodies David released were powerful enough to usher in heaven! Widespread revelation took place in the nation as people understood the power of prophetic music.

Saul, in jealousy, drove David to escape from the palace and flee to the prophet Samuel. Samuel lived in Naioth of Ramah, where he trained and raised up prophets and prophet musicians. Samuel rode on circuit to different places, but always came home to the place where he had built an altar for the Lord.

Samuel was leading a prophetic movement and creating a prophetic culture amidst the people of God. Samuel even prophesied to Saul about what had to come to pass before he became king of Israel.

> After that you shall come to the hill of God where the Philistine garrison is. And it will happen, when you

have come there to the city, that you will meet a group of prophets coming down from the high place with a stringed instrument, a tambourine, a flute, and a harp before them; and they will be prophesying. Then the Spirit of the Lord will come upon you, and you will prophesy with them and be turned into another man. (1 Samuel 10:5–6)

When Saul encountered this band of prophet musicians, he was changed into another man. God gave him a different heart!

This is the first time the word *band*, denoting a group of musicians playing together in unison, is used in any ancient literature. What a root that is for us to draw from! Musicians and artists are called to be prophets of the most high God.

When Saul encountered these prophets, he was awakened into his full calling and purpose. Without that encounter he did not have the credentials to be king.

The prophetic song brings encounter. One reason God is rebuilding the tabernacle of David today is so the rest of mankind can come to Him and have an encounter with the living God.

In the place of worship, His presence is found. In the place of prophetic song, encounter with a living God is eminent.

This Scripture says that a group of prophets was coming down from the "hill of God" where the Philistine garrison had a stronghold. This hill of God was Mount Zion. Mount Zion was a Philistine stronghold until David took it after he became king. This is where David built the tabernacle.

Our enemy will always contest the places of great destiny. This should give us hope for our cities and nations, no matter how dark they seem.

God had been sending bands of prophet musicians to

this contested stronghold for years before David took it for its intended purpose. God Himself was preparing that ground to be overtaken with His presence through prophetic worship years before David ever captured it.

The final key of understanding for David came when he fled to the prophet Samuel at his home in Ramah.

> David fled and escaped, and went to Samuel at Ramah, and told him all that Saul had done to him. And he and Samuel went and stayed in Naioth. Now it was told Saul, saying, "Take note, David is at Naioth in Ramah!" Then Saul sent messengers to take David. And when they saw the group of prophets prophesying, and Samuel standing as leader over them, the Spirit of God came upon the messengers of Saul, and they also prophesied. And when Saul was told, he sent other messengers, and they prophesied likewise. Then Saul sent messengers again the third time, and they prophesied also. Then he also went to Ramah, and came to the great well that is at Sechu. So he asked, and said, "Where are Samuel and David?"
>
> And someone said, "Indeed they are at Naioth in Ramah." So he went there to Naioth in Ramah. Then the Spirit of God was upon him also, and he went on and prophesied until he came to Naioth in Ramah. And he also stripped off his clothes and prophesied before Samuel in like manner, and lay down naked all that day and all that night. Therefore they say, "Is Saul also among the prophets?"" (1 Samuel 19:18–24)

Saul sent three groups of people to go get David. These were not conference-going Christians, but the king's mightiest men going to capture a man they saw as a fugitive. Each group was overcome with the power of the atmosphere created by David and got sucked into it.

After the first three teams failed, Saul himself went to do the job. He too fell down prostrate and prophesied all day and all night before Samuel.

Prophetic worship turns killers into prophets and kings into fools!

Saul was being used to paint a prophetic picture of the heavens on earth. He fell down and cast down his crown just as the elders in heaven will cast down their crowns. Not because Saul wanted to, but because he couldn't help it!

David put the pieces of this scenario together in his heart. Having seen the power of God in this, he knew he would establish 24/7 prophetic worship and praise to God once he became king. David had learned the power music carried. And if it could change men individually, it could surely change an entire nation!

Music Opens The Door

Music is rightly called the universal language. It is not only the common language of earth but also of the heavenly spiritual realm.

Right now, in the very abode and habitation of God Almighty, there is nonstop worship, with music and singing around the throne. It has always been this way and will always be this way. God's living room is constantly playing worship music! How right it is for music to be the vehicle upon the earth by which God encounters people and, through His eternal Word, changes the hearts of men.

A song will penetrate where a sermon will not. The heart is soft to the seed of melody, and its doors open to the sound of singing.

This is why God is raising up a singing church like never before, to usher in His word through song to bring great awakening to the earth. Paul testified of the power of music to the ancient Colossian church.

> Let the word of Christ dwell in you richly in all wisdom, teaching and admonishing one another in psalms and hymns and spiritual songs, singing with grace in your hearts to the Lord. (Colossians 3:16)

There is a new company of singing prophets upon the earth today. They are filled with the words of Christ and are singing prophetic songs over their generation.

Music is not merely the warm-up to the Word. Paul says that the church is to teach and admonish through all types of songs. He says we are to be filled in abundance with God's Word and then let it spill out in song and music to God. We can teach the word of God through singing! We can also admonish—to rebuke and even warn sternly. Music is not supposed to do away with preaching. But prophetic song greatly enhances sermons. Even Elisha called for the minstrel to come play so he could prophesy!

All people of every tribe and tongue have this in common: music. In whatever form and cultural affinity it may be, music is the soundtrack to our lives. In Exodus 32 God gave Moses the first prophetic song we see in the Bible. Then He told Moses to teach it to all Israel. Why? The same reason we teach our children the ABC song. Melody begets remembrance.

All creativity in music comes from God, but not all of God is in that creativity. Like any other good and powerful tool, music can be perverted over time.

Lucifer was the first worship director in heaven. His very

body was a musical instrument (Ezekiel 28:13). It makes sense that this most powerful force in the heavens and the earth is one of the most disputed territories we must battle over. Music has the ability to shift and define culture.

God wants the culture of heaven to invade the earth. Jesus prayed, "Let your kingdom come and Your will be done on earth as it is in heaven" (Matthew 6:10). We were all born of God. Our citizenship is in heaven, not of the earth. We are ambassadors from another realm, another kingdom. As pilgrims on the earth, the primary and natural overflow of our life work, in whatever specific and varied respect, should be to make this world look like the world we are from. In heaven, there is nonstop worship, praise, and singing to God. It makes sense, then, for us to do this same thing on the earth. His presence and kingdom are found upon it. God is enthroned on the earth, as in heaven, upon the praises of His people.

The difference between David and Saul was their hearts. David earned the title of having a heart after God (Acts 13:22). This fact was proved by his installation of night-and-day worship and adoration of God. The overflow of having God's heart can only be fully expressed in unending worship!

According to 1 Samuel 10 and 19, Saul had encounters with prophetic music and the powerful presence of God numerous times. However, these encounters were used selfishly instead of for others.

David knew the power of the presence of God and faithfully stewarded it unto an entire nation. His desire was that everyone would encounter the presence of God and live in a culture where the nearness of God was present. This is the tabernacle of David. And this is why God wants to rebuild David's tabernacle. He wants to raise up others who have His heart and build places of worship and prayer to Him where His presence can come and dwell.

The Lord wants whole cities, even whole nations, to be consumed in the power and goodness of His presence and glory. The kindness of God leads men to repentance.

The tabernacle of David will be restored so the multitudes can come to taste and see that He is good. The harvest that is coming will be caught up in the nets of the presence of God. The presence of God is the nearness of the very face of God Himself. When people see the beauty of His face, they will be forced to make a decision, either to follow or to oppose.

May His kingdom come and His will be done, on earth as it is in heaven! May we, like David, access God's heart and build a dwelling place upon the earth so that all people will know Him and His ways.

Chapter 9

MOUNT ZION'S KEY

God's heart is to have a people He can have relationship with. God desires worship, and He deserves it far more than we can ever know. Even the greatest theological discourse, or all of human wisdom, could not uncover the vastness of His goodness and worthiness to be worshipped. When we understand the beauty and worth of this man Jesus, our personal worship and our value for worshipping lifestyles will explode. The place of worship is a place of surrender, and surrender is one of the ultimate expressions of intimacy with God.

King David tapped into this form of worship as an overflow of his love for God. David's tabernacle was the culmination of his love and the revelation he had of worship. His desire to see God honored through worship was paired with the revelation of the power of praise and its relevance to the resting place of God's Spirit upon the earth.

The tabernacle of David was finally set up on Mount Zion, and it was the first form of worship in the old covenant that used the sacrifice of praise rather than the sacrifice of an animal. It captured God's heart, and He rested upon Mount Zion with His presence for thirty-three years as perpetual and unending songs, prayers, and thanksgivings were made directly to God. David had laid hold of a new-covenant reality in that he was tapping into the very essence of what God has always desired. Essentially, David's tabernacle is the picture of following the Spirit rather than the letter of the law.

If you are led by the Spirit, you are not under the Law. (Galatians 5:18)

David's tabernacle was the corporate overflow of his personal life. David seemingly broke the law and traditions as his love for God guarded him from the strict conditions and punishments the law would bring. He was a priest, a prophet, and a king. He represented the new-covenant believer, and his tabernacle was the corporate reality of his heart.

We do not need more kings on the hills of culture. Those who have not learned to be priests are not upon mountains for the glory of God, but for their own selfish glory. We need not play "King of the Hill." Trying to be the king of a mountain of culture is motivated primarily by the flesh. We don't need kings on the hill; we need priests in the secret place. Give me priests who know their God and I will show you a king who can exercise godly authority in the earth, to the will of the King of all Kings. God's kings have been trained in the secret place of prayer. They have learned to be servants. And they love His people more than they love themselves.

Even after he became king, Saul rarely sought God or leaned upon Him as his source of strength and help. Saul had encountered God's power in prophetic music. We see that in 1 Samuel 10 and 19. But Saul didn't steward his encounters as David did. Saul's encounters with God were selfish in nature, because unlike David, Saul never seemed interested in bringing the presence of God back to Jerusalem.

The reason is likely because Saul was a king before being a true worshipper or priest. David, on the other hand, had developed an intimate relationship with God, and this served to make him a godly king who could carry out the true will of the Father and be a Godlike representation as a leader to the people. In spite of David's faults, shortcomings, and sin, God favored him because of his humble and repentant heart. David was a good king because he was a faithful priest.

David brought heaven's reality to earth, and because of that the nation of Israel became blessed more than any other time in history.

The ark of the covenant was in the center of the tabernacle, and all could come to experience God's presence. David made the presence of God upon Mount Zion the central focal point of the nation and its culture. Because of this, David's son Solomon inherited the most blessed nation on planet earth. Israel enjoyed protection and victory in regard to their enemies, unending wealth, and most important, the very presence of God dwelling in the nation as a new generation grew up to experience the manifest presence of God.

David was extravagant when it came to offering worship to God. He hired the best musicians, he recruited the most anointed prophetic singers of his day, and he made sure that the fire on the altar never went out. David spent billions of dollars in today's currency toward building the tabernacle.

With this heart, God could trust David to such an extent that He promised him that His very own Son, the Messiah, would sit upon his throne. That is nothing to take lightly!

God will honor extravagant worship. He will honor and bless us today if we follow David's heart to be extravagant in our sacrifice for God.

Mount Zion: God's Dwelling on Earth

Mount Zion is where David pitched his tent and housed the ark of God. Mount Zion holds great significance for us today. Understanding its meaning in the Old Testament writings will give us great insight into God's plans today.

> The LORD will comfort Zion; He will comfort all her waste places. And her wilderness He will make like Eden, And her desert like the garden of the LORD; joy and gladness will be found in her, thanksgiving and sound of a melody. (Isaiah 51:3)

From Zion a garden will grow.

When Mount Zion is mentioned in the Old Testament, it speaks of the place where the tabernacle of David was. It would similar to Americans when they refer to Washington, DC. When we say, "There is turmoil and conflict in Washington," we are essentially saying, "There is turmoil in the government," because Washington, DC is where our federal government is located. Mount Zion was a place of nonstop worship and prayer, where the very presence of almighty God rested.

This is why Psalm 132 is a foundational Scripture to the worship-and-prayer movement. It declares how David swore an oath to the Lord that he would not rest, sleep, or slumber until he found a resting place for the Lord's presence on earth, a dwelling place for the Mighty One of Jacob. The Lord spoke over Zion these precious words and promises:

> The LORD has chosen Zion; He has desired it for His habitation. This is My resting place forever; here I will dwell, for I have desired it. (Psalm 132:13–14)

Mount Zion was known to the Israelites as the atypical "resting place" of God's Spirit on the earth and was thus referred to that way throughout the Scriptures.

> You have come to Mount Zion and to the city of the living God, the heavenly Jerusalem, and to myriads of angels. (Hebrews 12:22)

Mount Zion is the hill of the Lord and the mountain of God. Before David captured Mount Zion it was under the control of the enemy. The Philistines (which represent the flesh) had made a stronghold on this mountain. God had been sending prophetic bands of musicians there for years before David took the mountain and established its destiny as the resting place of God and the place of perpetual worship, prayer, and communion.

God is rebuilding Zion in His people and ultimately upon the earth. He wants us to build "Zions" in our homes, cities, and nations.

David's Key: The Key to Breakthrough

God is building up the tabernacle of David once again, and this time He is doing it with living stones (1 Peter 2:5, 9). Amos 9:11 and Acts 15:16 are foundational prophetic words that we must stand upon in order to be a part of what He is doing in these last days.

> In that day will I raise up the tabernacle of David that is fallen, and close up its breaches; and I will raise up its ruins, and I will rebuild it as in the days of old: That they may possess the remnant of Edom, and of all the nations, who are called by my name, says the LORD that does this. (Amos 9:11–12)

After this I will return, and will build again the tabernacle of David, which is fallen down; and I will build again the ruins thereof, and I will set it up: that the rest of men might seek after the Lord, and all the Gentiles, upon whom my name is called, says the Lord, who does all these things. (Acts 15:16–17)

These passages are the foundational call to the church to fulfill the rebuilding of King David's tabernacle. God will rebuild it as it was in the days of old.

In order to grasp what God is doing in this day, it's important to understand why God wants the tabernacle of David rebuilt in the first place. God wants His presence on the earth, and He wants all to be able to have access to it. King David made the tabernacle on Mount Zion accessible to all who wanted to come and experience God's presence. It was open to both Jews and Gentiles. God displayed His manifest presence and power in the place of worship and prayer and thus gave the unbelievers of that day an encounter with who He truly was.

God is rebuilding the tabernacle of David through people who have the heart of David. David discovered the power of a prophetic song to God. He unlocked God's heart in a way that no man had before. And by doing so, David found a key by which we turn our world into God's world, His kingdom coming to our earth. Isaiah 22:22 speaks of this key that opens and closes doors.

> Then I will set the key of the house of David on his shoulder, When he opens no one will shut, When he shuts no one will open. (Isaiah 22:22)

On whose shoulder does God set the key of David? Jesus Himself has this key. In Revelation 3:7 Jesus declares:

To the angel of the church in Philadelphia write: These are the words of him who is holy and true, who holds the key of David. What he opens no one can shut, and what he shuts no one can open. (Revelation 3:7)

A key's purpose is to open locked doors and lock closed doors. David's key was the revelation he had of God's heart concerning worship. David had tapped into what God has wanted all along: wholehearted, loving worship.

Jesus' authority is manifested through the place where we give Him room. This can be true individually and corporately. In a corporate sense we are the *ekklesia* of God; that is, the ruling and governing body of God's people who make decisions as to what is allowed and not allowed in the earthly realm. This power has been given to the church from on high. We must step into this authority humbly and confidently.

The heavens are open. The earth is what needs to be unlocked and opened. We are not trying to open the heavens. That was done when Jesus died on the cross and made a way for us. But the earth is closed, and this Scripture explains why:

The heavens belong to The Lord, but the earth He has given to mankind. (Psalm 115:16)

We are called to bring forth the will of God on the earth through relationship. We have the ability to open up the earth by using this key of David in the same way David did. He opened up the earthly realm in Jerusalem and in the nation of Israel by making a place for God to come and rule through the resting of His presence. If we make a place for Him to come rule, He will rule in our midst! This will happen not by our strength, but by His Spirit.

The LORD will stretch forth Your strong scepter from Zion, saying, "Rule in the midst of Your enemies." (Psalm 110:2)

Jesus rules and executes authority from His presence in Zion! David's key opens and closes doors in the spiritual realm, thus opening and closing doors in the natural. We recognize our identity as spiritual people who, using spiritual weapons, take dominion in the earth. David's key is a key to the heart of God, to bring His kingdom to earth through the resting of God's presence in a specific place.

David understood that when the presence of God is in your midst, you get all of the blessings associated therein. This would be similar to the richest man in the world joining your political campaign. You don't just get that man's support; you get all the money, resources, and influence he brings to the table by being a part of your team. You get more of that man's wisdom, insight, and help if you allow him to speak into the campaign. The same is true in any relationship.

When we get the presence of God, we get it all! When the presence of almighty God comes, *everything* it touches is blessed. When we have God's presence in our midst, we have the whole package.

This was true on an individual level for Moses, in a family context with Obed-Edom, and on a corporate and national scale with David and the nation of Israel. Moses carried God's presence upon his face, and he shone with the very glory of God. Obed-Edom had the resting place of God's presence in his home, and everything he had was blessed. David gave rest to God's presence through worship and prayer, and the entire nation was blessed because of it. We need His presence!

God's presence inhabiting our worship, praise, and prayers closes the doors of hell and opens the earth to receive heaven's blessings!

We must lay hold of the key of David for breakthrough in our day and for generations to come. In no other way will we be able to win the battle for the soul of our nations and coming generations. Our carnal weapons of winning a few souls here and there, or of having only earthly influence to try to bring about change, are coming to an end. This is a glorious thing. Earthly plans bring little fruit. God is beckoning us to test Him in this and take the land with the key of David!

Chapter 10

HABITATION OF GOD'S PRESENCE

As God begins to shift His church from a temporal to an eternal mind-set, we will see people sowing their lives into the ground of promise like never before. The body of Christ is awakening to the necessity of having God's presence upon us everywhere we go, not just in the church house. It can be seen, felt, and heard by all people, even unbelievers. We desire more than visitations in the church, whereby we have "revival" every so often when we grow weak and weary. What do we do when revival comes? Revival is unto a purpose and that purpose is still intended to follow God's order: ministry to God first, ministry to people second. Salvations, healings, miracles, and all the acts and works of God through His people are most definitely signs of revival. But what I am after is the saved, healed, and delivered to be true living stones, priests before their God and built up into a resting place of God!

I am all for revival. I believe we must always pray for it and contend to live in a place of revival. But what I speak of is deeper. We are not looking for visitation only, but habitation. God is not into one-night stands. He is after a bride. He wants more than

REVIVAL DEFINED [handwritten]

visitation rights to His children; He wants to abide with them. In fact, the habitation of God is the ultimate purpose of God for His people.

> Then I saw a new heaven and a new earth; for the first heaven and the first earth passed away, and there is no longer any sea. And I saw the holy city, new Jerusalem, coming down out of heaven from God, made ready as a bride adorned for her husband. And I heard a loud voice from the throne, saying, *"Behold, the tabernacle of God is among men, and He will dwell among them, and they shall be His people, and God Himself will be among them."* (Revelation 21:1–3, emphasis mine)

John the Revelator got a sneak peek into our ultimate destiny. I love how the New Living Translation puts this verse:

> I heard a loud shout from the throne, saying, "Look, God's home is now among his people! He will live with them, and they will be his people. God himself will be with them." (Revelation 21:3)

If a visitation of God's Spirit can be likened unto revival, then the habitation of His presence would most surely be likened to a global great awakening. While spiritual words can be confusing and too complex for edification at times, describing moves of God's Spirit is crucial for growth. The purpose of revival is multifaceted, yet it has a singular overall focus. That focus is to build up the resting place of God's Spirit upon the earth.

Revival winds bring building blocks. These building blocks are people, alive with the love of Jesus and eager to build Him

REVIVAL = RESTING PLACE [handwritten]

a place on the earth to rest. Ezra knew this when he prayed for revival.

> But now for a brief moment grace has been shown from the LORD our God, to leave us an escaped remnant and to give us a peg in His holy place, that our God may enlighten our eyes and *grant us a little reviving* in our bondage. For we are slaves; yet in our bondage our God has not forsaken us, but has extended loving kindness to us in the sight of the kings of Persia, *to give us reviving to raise up the house of our God, to restore its ruins* and to give us a wall in Judah and Jerusalem. (Ezra 9:8–9, emphasis mine)

It is biblical to pray for revival. However, Ezra prayed for reviving *unto* something. That something was to build the very resting place of God. Ezra prayed that God would give His people revival so that they could build a resting place for His presence: God's house, where worship and prayer would ascend from earth to the throne.

God wants to give us revival for complete cultural reformation. And He wants to give us personal revival so we will light afresh our commitment to live a lifestyle of worship and prayer. We are the living, breathing stones of God's altar upon the earth.

Paul said in Romans 12:1 that we ought to be living sacrifices. Living sacrifices are walking, moving altars where God puts His fire! Perhaps our greatest issue is that while we don't mind the fire, we often dislike buying the oil that keeps the fire going. If we want the habitation of God's presence in our midst, we must make our habitat a place where He is comfortable to rest. The symbolic nature of the oil and us being lamps cannot be overstated.

If we want the habitation of God's manifest presence and glory, we must be those who have the oil of true intimacy. Throughout the Bible oil represents the closeness and nearness of God's Spirit. A small flame with much oil that burns for many years is better than a large fire that is here today and gone tomorrow. God will always give the fire; it's our job to get the oil!

Building the Resting Place

We are the landing pads for God's presence, and corporately we are the gateway of heaven to earth. We are living stones and we are being built up *together*. We are so much better together than alone. Stones without a building to be placed into are no different from rocks. We are not living *rocks*; we are living *stones*. Stones are used for a specific purpose; rocks are not.

It should be said that rogue wanderers and wild stallions are useless in the kingdom of God. Even the most powerful men and women are no good unless they allow themselves to be built into the greater picture of God's plan. Stones are for the purpose of being used to build something greater than themselves.

> You also, as living stones, are being built up as a spiritual house for a holy priesthood, to offer up spiritual sacrifices acceptable to God through Jesus Christ. (1 Peter 2:5)

Our identity as living stones is tied into our purpose of being a holy, set-apart, royal priesthood, offering up prayer and worship to God. When the church comes alive in her purpose as a priest, she will be able to see the blueprint of the building God is constructing. When we spend time in God's presence, we will have light in our lamps to see "behind the scenes" and understand what God is up to. And rest assured, God is up to something! He is building a spiritual dwelling among His people that is impacting the globe.

One of the key Scriptures of this truth is found in Ephesians.

> ...having been built on the foundation of the apostles and prophets, Christ Jesus Himself being the corner stone, in whom the whole building, being fitted together, *is growing into a holy temple in the Lord, in whom you also are being built together into a dwelling of God in the Spirit."* (Ephesians 2:20–22, emphasis mine)

Like many men of old, Paul was an architect of God's plan among men. Paul called himself a wise master builder. He saw the heavenly blueprint, and he shows them to us here.

If you don't know the end result of the building you are constructing, you will have a difficult time achieving your plans. If we ignore our ultimate goal of hosting the very face and presence of God so that others may come to know Him, we will be forced to live in a building that wasn't made for the people of God.

Our plans and strategies are many, but we have forgotten our first love. We have built up many ministries and many people who cannot hold what they were called to hold: the very presence and glory of God Himself.

Ephesians 4:11–12 is often preached in reference to the five-fold ministry—the ministry of giftings upon leaders in God's body. Here is a foundational scripture for the five-fold ministry.

> And He gave some as apostles, and some as prophets, and some as evangelists, and some as pastors and teachers, for the equipping of the saints for the work of service, *to the building up of the body of Christ."* (Ephesians 4:11–12, emphasis mine)

God gave us these ministry gifts and callings for the equipping of the saints for the work of service. But if we stop there, we will merely raise up more ministers for the work of service. Learning how to do a particular ministry and serve people isn't a bad thing, but over time it cannot be sustained. Why? Because there is more to this Scripture! <u>We are to equip the saints for the work of service *unto the building up of the body of Christ*</u>.

This Scripture builds on the truth of Ephesians 2:20–22, which says that we are all being built up into a dwelling place for God's Spirit. God's end-time architects and engineers are to raise up a people of the first commandment. Wise master builders will equip us to be <u>priests to God</u> and <u>servant-kings to men</u>.

We cannot settle for outpourings of revival in this day. God is not into just "visiting" us in revival. He is looking for a place to stay! Our eyes should not only be on visitation, but on the habitation of His presence. This was the heart of King David when he proclaimed:

> O LORD, I love the habitation of Your house and the place where Your glory dwells. (Psalm 26:8)

Where we <u>make a place</u> for <u>God to stay</u>, we <u>make room</u> for His <u>power to be displayed</u>. The nation of Israel's greatest period of blessing came directly following David establishing 24/7 worship and prayer for thirty-three years. His son Solomon enjoyed wealth, protection, and blessing so great that the nations of the earth came to marvel at it.

God is ~~doing~~ calling people to pray and worship in this way again today. Isaiah 60:1–3 says that the glory of the Lord will rise upon us and kings will come to the brightness of our rising. Nations and kings will come to the resting place of God.

Now is the time to press into this revelation in our personal lives, our families, our cities, and the nations of the earth. Let this be our anchor as we build His resting place in every sphere of our lives. We are the building blocks that comprise this resting place. Without our individual lives hosting His presence, we cannot impact a whole city with His presence.

The principle Jesus spoke of when He said the gospel would be preached in Jerusalem, Judea, Samaria, and the uttermost parts of the earth (Acts 1:8), was one of focusing inwardly (our relationship with Jesus) and then outwardly (first commandment to second commandment). It starts individually and ends corporately. We love the one in front of us and burn for all nations to come to know Him. We love our families well and we intercede passionately for our cities.

If we are to be suitable bricks to build with in the places He has put us, we must make it our aim to make our lives a gracious host to His awesome presence. If we are faithful with little, He can do great and mighty things!

Let it be said of your life, your family, and your city and nation, that almighty God dwells therein. Sow your life into what He is building.

> Unless the LORD builds the house, they labor in vain who build it; unless the LORD guards the city, the watchman keeps awake in vain. (Psalm 127:1)

Chapter 11

DISCIPLING NATIONS IN THE PRESENCE

The scope of the church's calling is broad, yet the way to fulfilling it is narrow. Jesus has commissioned us with the daunting task of discipling whole nations (Matthew 28:19). At judgment day, God will separate discipled nations from unbelieving nations (Matthew 25:33). Whole nations and kings of nations will come to worship Jesus in the end. The Bible tells us that Jesus Himself is the desire of all the nations.

> I will shake all nations, and the desire of all nations shall come: and I will fill this house with glory, said the LORD of hosts. (Haggai 2:7)

Nations here can be translated "Gentiles." Jesus the Messiah is the desire of all Gentiles. Within every person and people group is the desire for Jesus Christ. All creation longs for the Son. Every religion is striving to know Jesus, whether they know it or not. With this in mind, we must move forward in boldness and clarity, understanding that when the earth experiences the presence and truth of who Jesus is, they will be drawn to repentance and come to know His redeeming love and, ultimately, salvation.

Jesus showed us how to disciple people in the kingdom of God on an individual basis. His focus was getting them to live a first-commandment lifestyle in everything they did: to know Him and love God. But what Jesus did with His disciples on an individual level, God had done with the Israelites on a national scale.

Jesus discipled individual believers in the presence of God. But how do we do this with whole churches or groups of people? How do we do this with movements and entire nations?

Churches are now springing up that will disciple people in the presence God. It is one thing to disciple people in doctrines and dogma. Many seminaries and Bible institutes do this well. Though in the midst of this, we have produced many people who know about God but do not know Him intimately and personally. Discipleship must include training in pure doctrine. But when following doctrine becomes more important than following God's Spirit, we are no longer sons and daughters but Pharisees.

There is no better example of discipling nations than how God discipled the Hebrew nation upon their exodus from Egypt. He took His people from despair, bondage, and slavery to the Promised Land full of inheritance. And the goal of their existence was to be priests and kings before Him, establishing His kingdom on the earth.

God's original intent with bringing His people out of their bondage to Egypt is seen in what He said through Moses to Pharaoh:

> Let my people go, *so that they may go* into the wilderness and worship Me. (Exodus 9:1, emphasis mine)

God desired worship: wholehearted love expressed through praise and thanksgiving. This reason was the reason they were delivered out of slavery. God was delivering them from slavery to freedom. The paradox here is that real freedom, in its truest sense, is being a willing slave to Him and to love.

God didn't want to force worship, or their love and trust. He delivered them into a place where He could show His great love for them, thus earning their trust and their worship. He did it through supernatural encounters and miracles.

The Lord always intends for His supernatural power to be displayed to a people in slavery. This miraculous power must be displayed to those who are in slavery to the god of this age. The Spirit of God brings freedom on every level; the presence of God in our midst breaks all the chains that bind us.

Where the spirit of the Lord is, there is freedom. (2 Corinthians 3:17)

The Lord wanted to bring the children of Israel into a worship lifestyle whereby His presence could lead them into all the promises of the covenant. God does the same today as He leads us from a place of slavery to the place of inheritance.

We must disciple individual people and entire nations in how to know and follow the presence of God. This is God's design. He led the freshly saved Hebrew people through the wilderness by teaching them to follow His presence. When the cloud by day and the fire by night stopped, they stopped. When His presence moved, they moved.

We too must follow His presence. We have even greater promises than the children of Israel when they came from Egypt. But our responsibility is also greater. We are to follow His presence and be led by the Spirit.

From the beginning, God wanted a family. He taught the children of Israel to follow His presence in the cloud by day and fire by night so they could be sons and daughters.

Those who are led by the Spirit of God are sons of God. (Romans 8:14)

Being a son or a daughter in the kingdom is directly linked to following and being led by God's Spirit.

The Lord brought the children of Israel out of Egypt and immediately established divine law in order to point them into a worshipping, first-commandment lifestyle, free from the slavery of idolatry. He established orders of worship so that His presence could dwell in their midst. Though the Jewish people often missed the heart of the matter, this was God's intent all along.

The same is true of the church today. The apostle Paul says that those who follow the Spirit of God are not under the law. The law was put in place as a boundary line to guide people to following the Spirit.

God asked the Israelites to create a place on the earth that mimicked His dwelling in the heavens. Moses made the tabernacle as a replica of the heavenly model (Hebrews 8:5). God doesn't dwell in what our ideas are of who He is. He dwells where we build a place on earth that mimics where He dwells in the heavenlies. We get into where God is at, not the other way around. God doesn't follow our presence; we follow His. We don't do something and ask God to be in it; we get into what He is doing!

The golden calf that the Israelites worshipped while Moses was on the mountain receiving the ten commandments was given the credit for what the Lord had done in Egypt. They worshipped this idol, thanking it for bringing them out of slavery, parting the Red Sea, and doing the mighty works that God did.

Our minds yearn to control what we know and to master knowledge. But God will not be put inside our molds. The greatness and majesty of God has to override our need to have control over knowledge and information about God. We must lean into and embrace the mystery of who He is. Only in our agreement with Him and His sovereign rule are we able to truly experience His leadership and freedom.

The Presence at the Center of It All

God brought a literal cloud by day and pillar of fire by night to His people. This was a manifest representation of the presence of God in their midst. God is doing this in His church today. He beckons us to follow the fire of His presence. May we, like the children of Israel. teach others to follow the presence of God, camp around the presence of God, and live our lives around it as the center of all we do.

David put the Presence in the center of the tabernacle, making it the central focus of the nation. After God's people were delivered out of their bondage and sin in Egypt, they had to learn to live life around the presence of God.

This is the model God wants to use for His church. There are many expressions and formats for this to play out, but one thing is certain: God's design is for His bride to live in His presence. Most American churches gather around a variety of things, most of which have little to do with the presence of God. We follow anointed preachers to hear great sermons. We talk about doctrines and methodology for how to do ministry. This is not always wrong. But if we are not focused on His presence being welcomed into our midst and being sensitive to what He is doing, we are missing the point of it all—His presence and nearness among us. When His presence leads, we follow. When His presence stops somewhere, we stop and camp around it.

Jesus led His inner circle of disciples—John, James, and Peter—to the top of a mount and He was transfigured before them, talking with Moses and Elijah. They basked in His presence and heard the audible voice of God. The disciples wanted to camp out there, but Jesus headed back down the mountain and they had to follow Him.

We cannot camp when He is moving. We cannot move when He is camping. Both are disobedience, and both put us in a dangerous place.

What if God's presence breaks outside our sacred Sunday-morning rituals? When we come together to worship, our purpose is not to have a good service or to provide a cool place for people; it is to welcome God in our midst and go where He goes. A revolutionary move of God is already happening in the church, where we are learning to follow and yield to His Spirit. If we do it together, we can follow Him when we are on the streets and in our everyday lives.

We would do better to teach new believers about the presence of God and following His Spirit than our favorite doctrines, which Bible translation to read, and other nonessentials. Knowing Jesus is knowing truth, and apart from this relationship and being led by Him we will be full of knowledge and empty of real love.

Perhaps new disciples would be better fit for changing the world if we taught them to simply "be with Jesus," like the disciples whom Jesus raised up, instead of herding them into Bible and seminary schools, where they are often taught their way out of the mystery of God and the childlikeness of true faith. We need a fresh movement of humble people who will teach believers to walk and abide in the presence of God. We are in need of a reformation in the church of Jesus Christ where we get back to our first love, unlearn our mastery of ministry, and follow the presence of God into lands of blessing and breakthrough yet unknown. By blessing and breakthrough I speak not just of the personal kind, but the blessing of a massive harvest of souls flooding into the kingdom. A breakthrough where dreamy-eyed revivalists shut the mouths of the wise of this age by winning and discipling entire nations unto God.

We are in need of a shift in our approach, and it is already under way as language and clarion calls are going forth for believers to not be "of Paul, or of Apollos," (1 Corinthians 3:4), but of the family of faith that recognizes God as their ultimate leader. Following the Presence will not upset honor, leadership, and godly authority in the church; rather, it will intensify true submissiveness and heartfelt humility based on love, not obligation.

A Presence-based church, city, or nation will be a place where prayer and worship is emphasized. We must have prayer and worship to maintain a culture in which Christ is at the center of everything. A Presence-based culture is a Christ-centered culture. Leaning into God, being dependent on Him for everything we do, honors the presence of the Lord in our midst and draws down God's strength where we would otherwise have only our own.

The worship and prayer movement is key to establishing and maintaining a Christ-central people. We are called to live in first-love fire. We do not pray, worship, and love upon the Lord *unto* something. The very thing we do in worship and prayer *is* that something. It is not the means to an end; it is the end. And that end is His presence in and upon us.

We cannot consistently live in God's face without being consistently changed into His image. Isn't this what we all desire—for Christ's image and character to be our own, where we can say as Jesus did that if you have seen us you have seen God?

Paul testified to this.

> But we all, with unveiled face, beholding as in a mirror the glory of the Lord, are being transformed into the same image from glory to glory, just as from the Lord, the Spirit. (2 Corinthians 3:18)

The Bible in Exodus 33:20 says that no one can see the face of God and live. A more proper rendering of this Scripture in the Hebrew is "You cannot see the face of God and live the same as you were before." When you make an intimate connection with God, you are changed. His life-giving breath and presence change us from the inside out. The chaff in you dies and God takes ground in your heart; you are His promised land!

Saul was changed into another man when he met the band of musical prophets who brought the presence of God into the earth (1 Samuel 10, 19).

Moses didn't die a natural death. His body was strong and healthy when the Lord took his life. Deuteronomy 34:7 says that His sight was good and body strong. In fact, the devil tried to get Moses' body (Jude 1:9). God hid the body of Moses, and no one could find it because it would have not decayed. Many theologians and scholars believe this happened when Moses' body was in the presence of God and supernatural life was pulsating through it. If the devil had gotten Moses' corpse into the hands of the Israelites, they would have turned it into an idol!

Just like Elisha's bones still had enough residue of God upon them to raise the dead, God wants us to be saturated in His presence. We must disciple people and nations in how to abide in the presence of God.

We must be a bride unto Christ who seeks to know His love and to be in love. A bride who is truly in love with her bridegroom will love his face. She will want to gaze into his eyes and always be with him. The same is true of the church and Christ. If we are to disciple nations we must lead them to God's presence and teach them to love His face.

Chapter 12

HEAVENLY MINISTRY AND CORNERSTONES

There are two primary ministries in heaven: the ministry of worship to God around the throne and the ministry of intercession.

As born-again believers, we are not of this world.

> But as many as received Him, to them He gave the right to become children of God, even to those who believe in His name, who were born, not of blood nor of the will of the flesh nor of the will of man, but of God. (John 1:12–13)

> Dear friends, I warn you as "temporary residents and foreigners" to keep away from worldly desires that wage war against your very souls. (1 Peter 2:11)

Hebrews 11 says this about the heroes of faith:

> These all died in faith, not having received the promises, but seeing them afar off and believing them and embracing them and confessing that they were strangers and pilgrims on the earth. (Hebrews 11:13)

We are from heaven, born from above through the blood of Jesus Christ and faith in Him. We are called to implant our culture (heaven) into this culture (the world).

Would it not make sense, then, that as foreigners living in a different land, we would continue to prioritize our services and ministry here the same way we would in our homeland of heaven? A people who migrate to different lands and nations, or pioneer into unknown lands, always take their culture with them. Culture goes deeper than conscious thought. It is so embedded in people's mind-sets and worldviews that its ways, traditions, and lifestyles are done without much thought. It's a part of who they are.

This is why, in places like New York City, there are so many people groups and cultures. All across America, we have Italian food, Mexican food, Mediterranean food, etc., because these pioneers brought their food styles with them.

God wants the culture of heaven to take dominion in the earth. This doesn't annihilate the beauty found in every indigenous people group. It simply brings to greater light and life the inherent culture those people groups already possess. It is like taking a black-and-white photo and making it color, with high definition and high resolution.

If we are to emulate the culture of our homeland of heaven, we must make the two eternal ministries of worship and prayer a foundational part of our lives and communities here on planet earth. Revelation chapters 4 and 5, as well as other parts of the Bible, give us insight into what is happening in heaven right now.

> Night and day they do not cease to say, "Holy, Holy, Holy is the Lord God, the Almighty, who was and who is and who is to come." (Revelation 4:8)

Night and day, for all eternity, the chorus and symphony of worship will be heard. It has been, is, and always will be worship that defines the lifestyle of heaven. It also defines the lifestyle of living life with God. Our worship is the sign of our relationship to God. Not in public only, but even more so in private. Our "homeland" of heaven has nonstop worship, and this worship is expressed in our homeland through music and song.

Prayer is also a vital ministry in heaven. Prayers have substance in the heavenly realm.

> When he had taken it, the four living creatures and the twenty-four elders fell down before the Lamb. Each one had a harp and they were holding golden bowls full of incense, which are the prayers of God's people. (Revelation 5:8)

The prayers of God's people manifest as incense in the spiritual realm. They can be seen and they even have a scent to them: a pleasing fragrance. The ministry of intercession is present in heaven.

As a matter of fact, Jesus Christ Himself is living, breathing, blood-pumping intercession and prayer, sitting on the throne of God.

> Jesus, on the other hand, because He continues forever, holds His priesthood permanently. Therefore He is able also to save forever those who draw near to God through Him, since He always lives to make intercession for them. (Hebrews 7:24–25)

This doesn't mean Jesus is constantly begging the Father to forgive us. That idea is an affront to His work on the cross and

His resurrection. In John 16:26 Jesus said He would not ask for anything from the Father on our behalf except that we would do that through Him.

When the writer of Hebrews says, "Jesus ever lives to make intercession for us," he means that Jesus' very life is a constant form of intercession, or "standing in the gap" on our behalf. Because He lives forever, we have a living, breathing intercession who sits at the right hand of God for us. Oh, how wonderful is our great high priest, Jesus the Messiah!

As the blood of Jesus cries out from the heavenly mercy seat and speaks a better word over us who have trusted in His name, we see that these two ministries are occurring in our native homeland and birthplace, heaven.

What happens when we implant the culture and ministries of heaven upon the earth? God's Spirit finds rest among us. We make the earth into a landing pad for His glory to come.

When we perform these primary ministries as priests on the earth to our God, we see that heavenly reality come forth on the earth.

It is time for us to stop trying to feed the world the "bread" they can get from anywhere, and feed them the bread of heaven. We owe it to them to make resting places of the presence and power of God on earth so that they may hear, see, and taste that He is good!

This is a part of how the tabernacle of David will bring in a great harvest. No one can argue against the raw power and glory of God!

Let the world see a burning church once again. Not consumed with outward political agendas, but a burning lamp to the entire world, in love with their God!

God is setting His people in place to build this dwelling place of His presence on the earth for all men to see. We must follow after our Cornerstone to know what is required of us.

Jesus, the Cornerstone

> You also, as living stones, are being built up as a spiritual house for a holy priesthood, to offer up spiritual sacrifices acceptable to God through Jesus Christ. For this is contained in Scripture: "Behold, I lay in Zion a choice stone, a precious corner stone, and he who believes in Him will not be disappointed. This precious value, then, is for you who believe; but for those who disbelieve, the stone which the builders rejected, This became the very corner stone." (1 Peter 2:5–7)

The cornerstone concept is derived from the first stone set in the construction of a masonry foundation. It is of utmost importance because all other stones will be set in reference to this stone, thus determining the position of the entire structure.

Jesus is the chief cornerstone. Everything we do as believers is modeled after His life and character. His acts, ministry, and words in the New Testament are the very essence of who God is and how we are to live. Our understanding of Him affects the way we do everything in life.

It is foolish to build a structure without first knowing what the end result will be. No architect would begin construction without knowing where the cornerstone was in relation to his building. We are foolish to build upon any foundation other than Christ. Christ is our cornerstone.

Jesus is also our High Priest. God is restoring the tabernacle of David, which represented the royal priesthood who ministered praise to God. God surrounds Himself in His heavenly home with praise, adoration, and worship. When the church, God's people, begins to look like the church in heaven, we will see the kingdom come to earth like never before. Heaven's domain, with all its blessing and provision, will break into the darkest and hardest places. Where there were demonic strongholds, a new principality will be proclaimed: the Prince of Peace, King Jesus!

From the place of the priesthood, we will rebuild the tabernacle of David. The more living stones, the greater the resting place.

The Bible speaks of believers as living stones. We are spoken of as pieces in a puzzle, or blocks in a larger building or structure. God is building us up into something greater and more wonderful than we could ever be on our own. He is making us into a resting place for His presence on earth.

> So then you are no longer strangers and aliens, but you are fellow citizens with the saints, and are of God's household, having been built on the foundation of the apostles and prophets, Christ Jesus Himself being the corner stone, in whom the whole building, being fitted together, is growing into a holy temple in the Lord, in whom you also are being built together into a dwelling of God in the Spirit. (Ephesians 2:19–22 NASB)

Jesus Himself is the foundational stone whereby all other stones are placed. And Scripture says:

> Thus says the Lord GOD, "Behold, I am laying in Zion a stone, a tested stone, a costly cornerstone for the foundation, firmly placed. He who believes in it will not be disturbed." (Isaiah 28:16)

The foundational stone of the building that all believers are being built up into is located in Zion, the dwelling place of God! That place represents not only the resting place of God's presence but also where night-and-day worship and prayer will be.

The cornerstone is in David's tent!

If we would grasp this simple truth, it would change everything that we set our sights on as the Church of Jesus Christ. The building's foundation is Christ the cornerstone. Our foundation is in Zion, the place of the presence of God and the place of perpetual praise and worship.

> We are "living stones, being built up as a spiritual house for a holy priesthood, to offer up spiritual sacrifices acceptable to God through Jesus Christ" (1 Peter 2:5).

How can the church come into alignment with the cornerstone without understanding where the cornerstone is and where it has been placed? How can we come into agreement with our spiritual identity unless we understand the nature of our ultimate assignment: to be a holy priesthood who offers up spiritual sacrifices? This is the rebuilding of the tabernacle of David.

God could live anywhere He wants, but He has chosen Zion. This is the place where He will dwell in the midst of praise, worship, and prayer (Psalm 132).

Our cornerstone is the eternal High Priest of God from the tribe of Judah, the tribe of praise. God is enthroned as King on our praise. It is the most fitting way to build a throne in the earthly realm for Him to come sit on.

> "You have made them to be a kingdom and priests to our God; and they will reign upon the earth." (Revelation 5:10)

Our reigning is directly related to our priesting. The degree to which we prioritize worship and prayer, the lifestyle of a priest, is the amount of authority we will have to reign.

Kingdom reigning is different from earthly ruling. Kingdom authority serves through love. Our intimacy with God will determine the extent to which we can serve and love others.

Building spiritually as priests will cause us to see the manifestation in the natural as kings.

Jesus is the foundation for everything we build. Paul said, in his letter to the Corinthian church, that every work will be tried by fire, and those works that are built upon Christ will remain but those that were not will be burnt up.

> According to the grace of God which was given to me, like a wise master builder I laid a foundation, and another is building on it. But each man must be careful how he builds on it. For no man can lay a foundation other than the one which is laid, which is Jesus Christ. Now if any man builds on the foundation with gold, silver, precious stones, wood, hay, straw, each man's work will become evident; for the day will show it because it is to be revealed with fire, and the fire itself will test the quality of each man's work. If any man's work which he has built on it remains, he will receive a reward. If any man's work is burned up, he will suffer loss; but he himself will be saved, yet so as through fire. (1 Corinthians 3:10–15)

Paul was a wise master builder. Everything he built was in relation to the cornerstone: Christ. The foundation of all that we build upon must be God's presence. We must build upon Jesus in the midst of His people through communion with Him.

> His *foundation* is in the holy mountains. The Lord loves the gates of Zion More than all the other dwelling places of Jacob. (Psalm 87:1–2 NASB, emphasis mine)

The Lord dwells in the midst of a people who long to praise Him and love Him from a thankful heart.

Paul was a skilled church planter, and the foundation on which he built was the presence of God. He would surely have taught on the Shema (to love God with all you have) and its full reality through the finished work of the cross of Christ.

While I love to look at the early church and their work, they did not corner the market on the "best" way to "do church." I don't want to have a first-century church. Older isn't always better. We can glean from the way they did things in hopes of seeing a purity that may not be present today. But the principle is what must be obtained. God didn't intend for the early church to have all the fun and leave the rest of the church's history playing catch-up to what they already attained. No, He intended for us to discover the "new-old" things of His heart and implement them by the wisdom and revelation He is releasing today.

We actually dishonor the works of Paul and the early church by making their works the high-water mark instead of pressing into the greater things God has for us. We honor them by moving into the new horizons God is calling us to. We carry the heart of Paul and the Scriptures by being pioneers. Paul said, "Thus I aspired to preach the gospel, not where Christ was already named, so that I would not build on another man's foundation" (Romans 15:20).

The great cloud of witnesses cries out for us to go further and believe for more. God Himself desires for us to make the earth into a garden again—a place where He is welcomed, where life is abundant, and where people eat from the tree of the living God, not just come up with good ideas born from the tree of the knowledge of good and evil.

Chapter 13

THE GOVERNMENT OF THE PRESENCE

For unto us a Child is born, unto us a Son is given; and the government will be upon His shoulder. And His name will be called Wonderful, Counselor, Mighty God, Everlasting Father, Prince of Peace. Of the increase of His government and peace there will be no end, upon the throne of David and over His kingdom, to order it and establish it with judgment and justice from that time forward, even forever. The zeal of the LORD of hosts will perform this. (Isaiah 9:6–7)

Perhaps one of the most beautiful and articulate Scriptures regarding Jesus is found in the writings of Isaiah. In chapter 9 Isaiah says that the Son of God will hold the government upon His shoulder. The Messiah will sit upon the throne of David. And there will be no end to the increase of His government and of His peace.

Government refers to the ruling body of a nation or kingdom. Jesus will carry all rule and authority of the kingdom of God upon His shoulder. All of the kingdom of God upon the earth is established and held up by Christ, the Son of God, the Word of God.

In this Scripture we see an interesting truth. The presence of

God, represented in the ark of the covenant in the Old Testament, could only be carried on the shoulders of God's priests. The Jews in Isaiah's day understood that meant that the Son of God would be a priest. The Messiah would carry the presence of God; therefore, He would also carry governmental authority.

Jesus had authority to heal the sick, raise the dead, perceive the minds of men, walk on water, and do other signs, wonders, and miracles because He carried the presence of God.

To carry God's presence is to walk in an abiding lifestyle. It means to constantly "stay in God's face." Carrying the presence means you carry governmental authority. Intimacy with God brings authority.

Jesus taught us how to live. He is our High Priest. All those who believe on the name of Jesus and are born again are priests unto God. We model our High Priest, Jesus, in all ways.

God's government is founded upon the Word of God (Jesus), expressed through the nearness and reality of His manifest presence. The "letter" of God's Word leads us to the "life" of God's Word, who is Jesus Christ Himself. God has founded His kingdom on Christ and His works.

> You search the Scriptures, for in them you think you have eternal life; and these are they which testify of Me. But you are not willing to come to Me that you may have life. (John 5:39–40)

God's government is found in the place of His presence. Throughout the Word, the Father prophesied of His Son, who would rule from the place of the presence.

> "But as for Me, I have installed My King upon Zion, My holy mountain." (Psalm 2:6)

Jesus rules as King from Zion, the place of worship and prayer. God reigns from the place where His presence is welcomed to come and rest. God wants us to build Him a resting place on earth so that He can also have a ruling place on earth.

The type of ruling authority I speak of is not as the world sees ruling. Ruling in the kingdom of God is the opposite of ruling in a worldly understanding. God rules by serving. Greatness in the kingdom of God is found in serving, not in being served.

> Calling them to Himself, Jesus said to them, "You know that those who are recognized as rulers of the Gentiles lord it over them; and their great men exercise authority over them. But it is not this way among you, but whoever wishes to become great among you shall be your servant." (Mark 10:42–43)

We want to build a resting place of God's presence through worship and prayer so He can have a ruling place to serve cities and nations.

The Lord wants to establish justice in the earth and to see men come to repentance.

Jesus is enthroned in the praises of His people. Look again at Isaiah's detailed prophecies concerning this.

> A throne will even be established in loving-kindness, and a judge will sit on it in faithfulness in the tent of David. (Isaiah 16:5)

Jesus' kingship is most rightly manifested on earth through the place of His presence in Zion.

> "The LORD will stretch forth Your strong scepter from Zion, saying, "Rule in the midst of Your enemies." (Psalm 110:2)

Zion is synonymous with the tabernacle of David, the place of worship, praise, and prayer. God says from Zion Jesus will stretch forth His scepter, His authority, and rule in the midst of our enemies. Beloved of God, this is a promise. And now is the time to build! As we make earth look like heaven, we give God full reign to execute justice. In heaven we see God's perfect and complete control. Worship is a weapon on the earth!

Bowing down and worshipping characterize the high court of heaven. *Worship* means "to bow down." The Supreme Court of heaven is completely and unashamedly apprehended with worship. The government of heaven is exhibited through the saints' worship on the earth. The psalmist affirmed this in singing, "He is enthroned on the praises of His people." God sits as king among His people's worship.

What is the government of God? It is His presence on the earth, carried on the praise and worship of new-covenant priests. After all, our High Priest is not from the tribe of Levi (the law) but from the tribe of Judah (praise)!

This is the cornerstone of the building we are all a part of. This is the resting place of God on the earth, and we are the living stones of this great altar. God has cut past the rule-based part of our ministry and gone straight to the core of the matter: our hearts!

Any pilgrim planting his culture in a different place knows that some sort of governmental system must be established to maintain a sense of order and justice. We are pilgrims from heaven, and where we come from there is 24/7 worship. We are to establish in our homes, churches, cities, and nations the culture of a worshipping lifestyle. When we establish worship, we establish His presence as the reigning authority over everything else. Devils flee, demonic strongholds are weakened and torn down, and Jesus takes His rightful place as ruler over all the kings of the earth.

Satan was cast down from the place of worship. Even today, when worship goes forth in a place or region, the demons have to leave!

The praises of the nation of Israel under King Jehoshaphat brought forth the Lord as a mighty warrior who ruled and fought for His people. They had victory that day because of their worship and praise, not their strong army (2 Chronicles 20).

Isaiah 42:10–13 says that when we sing the new song of the Lord in worship, God will go forth like a warrior, arouse His zeal like a man of war, and shout as He gains victory over our enemies.

God exercises complete authority and rulership in heaven. He wants to do this through His beloved bride upon the earth. A part of doing this is creating a culture of heaven on earth.

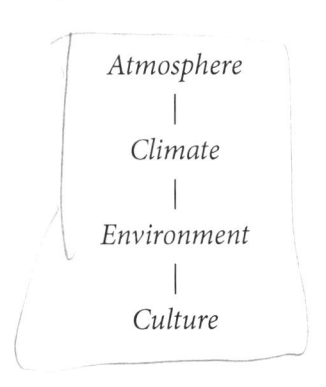

Atmosphere
|
Climate
|
Environment
|
Culture

The above diagram is a simple way of showing how the spiritual atmosphere of regions can be changed through sustaining God's presence. This can be applied individually or corporately.

If you sustain an atmosphere, you will reap a climate.

If you sustain a climate, you will reap an environment.

If you sustain an environment, you will reap a culture.

We start out with atmosphere. An atmosphere can change

quickly. It can be cold in the morning, hot in the middle of the day, and cold again at night.

When an atmosphere is sustained long enough, it is considered a climate. This speaks of a sustained atmosphere where a certain temperature is consistently maintained. Climate doesn't change as often as an atmosphere. It is generally referred to in seasons. In the summer the weather is hotter. In winter, the weather is colder.

When a climate is sustained for long periods of time, it creates an environment. An environment remains the same for even longer periods. Oranges won't grow in Ohio, but they will in Florida, because the overall temperature in Florida remains more constant than in Ohio. The same is true of the habitation of animals in the rain forest that would not survive in colder regions where a climate is not sustained.

The same is true of spiritual matters. Some things will not grow in a particular environment. Some fruit cannot be grown without an environment of His presence.

What is the overall spiritual "temperature" of our lives, our churches, our cities and nations? Nothing raises the heat of the spiritual condition of individuals and regions more than prayer and worship.

When we sustain an environment for long enough, a culture develops. Culture goes deeper than thought. Culture is a way of thinking that precedes rational thought. Culture is built into the way a group of people think, and they can't always explain why.

God wants a culture of heaven to invade the earth where miracles, signs, and wonders are normal. Where healings and deliverance are daily occurrences. Where the glory of God is so evident that even the hardest heart is broken down by His majesty and power.

To take down principalities, or a network of demonic strongholds over regions, we need to work in the opposite spirit and build a higher and larger principality. Any kingdom gains ground when its influence is dominant in a given area. We must build a principality of the presence of Jesus Christ in our cities and nations. We must pioneer a resting place for God so that His rule and dominion can come. We must carry the presence of the Lord so that we have the authority to destroy the works of the devil and declare justice in the land.

Part Three

The Mission

Chapter 14

JESUS, THE PIONEER MISSIONARY

Jesus was the original pioneer missionary. He left the grandeur, beauty, and comfort of heaven to come to earth as a man. His assignment in that foreign land was to tell us to repent because the kingdom of God was at hand. His mission was clear: to restore man to fellowship with God, fulfilling the law we could not attain to. He was the perfect Lamb, slain for the sins of the world. He was the God-Man who came not only to be crucified, to die, and to rise from the dead, but to show us how to live and how to love.

But Jesus was not doing a one-time, short-term mission trip to earth. He did not come one time and then withdraw, leaving us as orphans to find the way. He is the author and the finisher of our faith. Jesus is faithful to the work He's been given, and He will complete the work He has started in us (Philippians 1:6). This is the work of a true pioneer missionary.

When Jesus finished His time on earth, He sent the Holy Spirit to live inside the heart of every born-again believer, to finish the work He started. He promised He would be with us even until the end of the age (Matthew 28:20). The mystery of all the ages is that Christ lives in us (Colossians 1:27).

Not many people will leave the comforts of their own homes and cultures in obedience to the Lord's leading. Throughout history, missionary movements to spread the gospel around the world have been done by the faithful few. But God doesn't need the masses. Gideon's three hundred, the nation of Israel being priests for the whole world, and even Jesus' twelve disciples all accomplished the work of God.

Fewer still will give their lives to pioneer in a place until it comes into its full potential. Jesus is our great example.

The apostle Paul knew of this type of pioneering. He had a heart to pioneer the gospel and the presence of God where it had never been known. In Romans 15:20 he said, "I go where no man has built before, where none have heard the gospel so that I wouldn't build on another man's work." A generation will be marked by how well they carry God's face with them to the ends of the earth. This is the heart we must take with us when breaking new ground, and even keeping old ground occupied.

Jesus' love compels Him to stay with us through the good and the bad, the hard and the easy times. His love will compel us to go to and even stay in some of the darkest places on earth, contending for His presence to be known among all men.

Jesus will continue to live in His people until the fullness of Christ is formed in them, even until the last breath. He is pioneering in His people even today, taking new ground in the hearts of men and women. He goes into uncharted territory, establishing His rule and reign. He fights for the landscape of our souls to establish them as a place of the presence of God.

This is our calling as well.

When Christ comes to live inside the heart of the believer, it could be said that though He has "taken the land" of that person's life. Yet there is more of us that He desires. He is not satisfied

JESUS, THE PIONEER MISSIONARY

with a portion of us. He wants it all, and He will stop at nothing until He has it. Much like the children of Israel taking the promised land, Jesus in the same way takes our hearts and lives as His promised land. What a wonderful reality to know that right now you are Jesus' promise and the reward of His suffering. Jesus wants and deserves every part of our lives.

He is both kind and fierce in His approach to winning the fullness of our hearts. He is both merciful and jealous in His attack on the bondage that binds us. He came that we may experience abundant life (John 10:10). This attitude of Christ in our lives must translate into our work in the places God takes us. What if we had the same determination to see the fullness of God's destiny manifest in our cities and nations as Christ does for His people?

Pioneering a place for the presence of God isn't for the sake of always being on the cutting edge. It is for the purpose of establishing a settlement where people can build and a culture can be lived out. Men don't pioneer in the arts or science without a purpose. They strive to open the door for others to come through and live in that breakthrough. This is true for us, too, as we build the culture of heaven on the earth. The purpose of pioneering isn't to say you've "been there." True pioneering is occupying the places you've gone to. God wants to build upon the foundation of Jesus Christ, His precious cornerstone.

There is a difference between pioneering and wanderlust. One serves long-term goals and the other serves short-term, selfish desires.

We must change our priorities in this generation that wants to experience adventure. God will take you to places you never dreamed of if you give yourself to Him.

Many young people today are dedicated to seeing their

hometowns become all God intended them to be. And this has been the launching pad to other dreams of their hearts. They wonder, *Why did God put me with this family?* Or, *Why did God put me in this town, in this nation?* The answer is that we are all put where we are to be a terror to the gates of hell and to set up a resting place of the presence of God.

In the book of Acts, Simon the Sorcerer offered to pay money to have the "super-apostles" of his day lay hands on him so that he could have what they had. He earnestly desired their influence and the power operating in their lives. The apostles told him it didn't work that way, and that evil in his heart had caused him to ask such a thing.

We think that superior training from the great leaders in the best schools will qualify us to do the same great acts. But true authority cannot be bought, nor can it be taught. It comes only from being obedient, growing in intimacy, and being faithful to the call of God on our lives.

We can receive many things from leaders, but intimacy is not one of them. At best we should seek the same hunger and desire that rests on their lives. Men can give us fire, but they cannot give us oil. Learning to cultivate the oil of intimacy with God is paramount in determining the power and longevity of our inward flames that cause us to shine with power.

Muscle comes from resistance. Muscles build in a person when they are exercised and continually pushed past their comfort level. In fact, muscle actually tears and is broken down and then builds up more upon what was there before.

The same is true with spiritual muscle. There is no school or training in the world that can work out our spiritual muscles more than a continual walk in the school of Holy Spirit. This isn't to disregard or disrespect schools, training centers, and the like.

In fact, they are necessary, just as a good workout program is necessary for proper athletic training. But without experiencing the subtle drudgery that comes from plowing in our backyards or places that are not yet booming spiritual epicenters, we ultimately become very busy without doing a whole lot for ourselves or for others.

Jesus' work in us as the church is to make us a dwelling place of God on the earth, walking carriers of His presence and power. The goal of God is to conform us into the image of His Son. He fights without ceasing to renew our minds unto the mind of Christ and to make our lives ground zero for His Spirit to touch the earth. The Lord doesn't give up on us when we are stubborn and don't obey. He doesn't grow weary with us after continual failure. His patience in our lives and His mercy toward us is the testimony of His great commitment to us. Should we be any different inside the families, cities, and nations where God has placed us? The Holy Spirit pioneers a place for God in our lives, and we are to pioneer a place for Him in the earth. This is the beauty of the inner and the outer intertwined and working together.

I am glad that Jesus doesn't choose people who are the best looking and the most fun. Many of us would be out of luck in that scenario. I love that Jesus chooses the foolish and the weak to move through. He chooses the foolish things to confound the wise (1 Corinthians 1:27(. He even chooses the foolish places. God chose to have His Son born in little Bethlehem in a cold, dirty barn. Jesus was from Nazareth, and many people of His day asked, "What good comes out of Nazareth?" He hung out in a nowhere place like Bethany, and He continues to move all over the world in the strangest of places. No one is too small to be used, and no place too bad.

Where are the laborers to the Islamic nations?

Where are the pioneers to the Asian peoples?

What about the dry religious places of America, or the large cities riddled with debauchery? Where are the burning, shining lamps?

They are coming from the commitments held by God's people within the places He has put them. They will be married to the dream of God for their land and its people.

These pioneers are saying no to hopelessness. They are divinely naive as to what they are up against. Their childlikeness will open the door to great blessing and favor as they do what people said could not be done. Pray that God will raise up the pioneers of His presence and confound the wisdom of this age!

Digging in Desert Lands

Psalm 84 is the pioneering manifesto.

> How blessed is the man whose strength is in You, in whose heart are the highways to Zion! Passing through the valley of weeping they make it a spring; the early rain also covers it with blessings. They go from strength to strength, every one of them appears before God in Zion. (Psalm 84:5–7)

Blessed are those whose hearts have a destination. Highways are roads that lead to places. Those who have their hearts set on Zion, the place of the presence, are blessed. Zion is the place of the manifest presence of God, where He rests and dwells. Those who have their sights set on the presence of God will go through the dry valley, the valley of sorrows and weeping, and make it a spring. They will go through desert lands and turn them into gardens. They go from strength to strength and glory to glory, and they reach their destination of Zion, appearing before God Almighty. What a promise!

God wants the desire of our hearts to be Him; specifically, His presence. He wants heaven on earth. He wants our hearts to be set on the city of God, the city of the King, Mount Zion. Our individual journeys take different paths and turns, but one thing that binds all Christians together is that we are seeking to make this world look like His. Whether that is seen through giving a drink of water to the thirsty or performing miracles for the helpless, when we bring His presence we bring heaven to earth!

Those who know the power of the presence will pioneer in the hardest and darkest of lands, knowing that they hold the power to bring change through prayer and worship.

I am living to make the dry desert places rivers and springs after I go through them. I will change the places of weeping into places of singing and joy. I believe that my sons and daughters will know a different reality than I do now.

The presence of God should be growing from generation to generation in our families and cities. The desert lands of today should be the rain forests of tomorrow. Where the things of God were scarce, life will soon abound!

Hebrews testifies of the pioneers of faith in chapter 11, which closes with this timeless remark:

> "And all these, having gained approval through their faith, did not receive what was promised, because God had provided something better for us, so that apart from us they would not be made perfect." (Hebrews 11:39–40)

The pioneers of yesterday lived, in essence, for the pioneers of tomorrow. We honor our mothers and fathers in the faith by pressing into the unknown, as they did. We live for a generation we may never see. We are the walking promise of generations gone by. We are the prophetic fulfillment of countless words, promises, and dreams of yesterday. The goal is that we walk in a better world than they dreamed of that we may complete their work.

Jesus is wooing us into the wilderness of the narrow way and to the dark places. The true pioneer Himself wants to lead you down the road less traveled. Hear His voice, and follow His lead!

Chapter 15

TURN THE WORLD UPSIDE DOWN

We have been charged by the Word of God to turn the world upside down. While this phrase has become a cliché, we must not discount it. God truly has called us to change the world with our lives. Our time as pilgrims here on earth is to be spent in such a way that we leave it better than before we came. For those who call themselves followers of Christ, our call is to advance the reign and dominion of His kingdom in every way possible. Big acts and small alike are to the end that Christ's kingdom is advanced. As the Bible says, "The kingdoms of the world will become the Kingdoms of our Lord and His Christ" (Revelation 11:15).

The ways of making Christ's kingship evident in the earth are broad. The "big things" do not necessarily have the greatest impact. In fact, in the kingdom of God, the small things can have the greatest impact. Jesus spoke of this when he talked of the kingdom of God being like a mustard seed, which is the smallest of all seeds but when planted grows into the largest of all trees in the garden.

I am convinced that the "big things" we do in ministry or in life are usually less impressive to heaven than everyday acts of love. Some of the things that are highly esteemed in man's eyes are detestable in the sight of God.

We are often deceived when it comes to what truly matters to God. Our head knowledge of God can rob us of understanding His heart in an intimate way. We desire to advance His kingdom, so we desire to do great acts in His name. This is good, and God will perform great exploits through us. But it is the foolish things that will captivate heaven, enthrone Jesus as King in our lives, and advance His rule in the earth. Jesus performed the greatest act of ministry of all time by dying on the cross, redeeming man to God. This great act of ministry was watched by few, applauded by none, and more humiliating than we will ever know on this side of eternity. Yet it yielded the greatest results that will ever be known or perceived by the human heart.

Acts 17:6 says:

> When they could not find them, they dragged Jason and some of the brothers before the city authorities, shouting, *"These men who have turned the world upside down have come here also.* (emphasis mine)

Paul and Silas, on their second missionary journey, went to Thessalonica and stayed in the house of a man named Jason. When the Jews in the city heard they were coming, they incited a riot against them, saying, "These are the guys who have turned the world upside down, and now they're coming here!" They had just come from a prison in Philippi, which was about seventy miles from Thessalonica, the capital city of Macedonia. According to Acts 16:25–26, Philippi was where Paul and Silas were beaten and put in prison, and they sang songs so loud and prayed so thankfully and fervently that a mighty earthquake shook the prison foundation and opened all the prison doors and caused every chain to fall off. News of this, and probably many other exploits, had surely traveled to the men who took them to the city authorities and accused them of "turning the world upside down" in Thessalonica too.

How they did it is found in Acts 17:7:

Jason has received them, and they are all acting against the decrees of Caesar, *saying that there is another king, Jesus."* (emphasis added)

Whether through preaching, teaching, singing, or praying, their missionary journeys and their total lifestyle had one central theme: Jesus is King.

This simple, yet profoundly controversial theme has been and always will be at the core of the advancing church, the *ekklesia* of God, who restores cities and disciples nations in the way of the Lord—the ruling body in the earth that brings the kingdom of heaven to the kingdoms of this earth, bringing righteousness, peace, and joy in the Holy Spirit.

David knew this concept well. Surrounded by nations with huge armies, great kings, and massive lands, David boasted in his God by setting up night-and-day worship whereby nonstop, around the clock, it would be proclaimed, "Our God is King of all the earth and He deserves all the glory!" In tiny Israel, David proclaimed that Yahweh was the King of Kings and Lord of all other lords. This simple revelation that David lived by procured the greatest and most blessed time in all of Israel's history, even until this very day. David modeled heaven in that there was nonstop communion, praise, thanksgiving, and worship to God in his tabernacle. This truth is found in Psalm 22:3:

"You are holy, O You who are enthroned upon the praises of Israel."

The New Living Translation says it this way:

"You are holy; you sit as king receiving the praises of Israel."

God is fully enthroned in the heavens, with full control and reign, and He wishes it to be the same on earth through His saints. God delights in co-laboring with His sons and daughters through relationship, to bring about His will. He is making the earth into a garden again, and He is doing it in large part by making the church on the earth look more like the church in heaven.

When we give praise and worship to God, He is enthroned upon that place of adoration. Jesus' kingship is most rightly seen on the earth through the worship and praise of His people on the earth. It seems foolish to think that the Lord's kingship can be manifested on the earth through simply worship and prayer; yet that is the very way that the Lord has used throughout the Bible and church history to bring forth advancement in His kingdom whereby heaven comes to earth.

God is turning the world upside down in our day. Upside down to those who are not in line with His kingdom, and right side up for those who are.

The early church had far less in the way of materials and resources than we do to grow in God. But what they lacked in materials they made up for in the power of the Holy Spirit. Our modern-day church abounds in teachings, books, and many Bibles, including the New Testament. Yet we suffer from poor obedience and little power.

But I believe a corporate change is among us. We will turn the world upside down. The early church's exploits we read about in the book of Acts are not the high mark. They are not even the goal. The early church was only the starting place!

A global worship and prayer movement is sweeping the earth. Not in just one place, like in the days of the Moravians of Hernhutt or the Celts in Ireland, but in every nation. Incense is arising and the fulfillment of Malachi 1:11 is dawning in our day. Jesus is being proclaimed as King through the songs and declarations of singing prophets. The world is being shaken and stirred as Jesus is declared King, and His kingship is made evident through His prevailing presence and glory that will be found in His resting places across the earth.

The Highest Mountain

> "Now it shall come to pass in the latter days that the mountain of the Lord's house shall be established in the top of the mountains, and shall be exalted above the hills; and people's shall flow to it. Many nations shall come and say, "Come let us go up to the mountain of the Lord, to the house of the God of Jacob; He will teach us His ways and we shall walk in His paths. For out of Zion the law shall go forth, and the word of the Lord from Jerusalem."

Both Micah 4 and Isaiah 2 prophesy about the mountain of the Lord's house. The Lord's house is the house of prayer, and this mountain where He dwells is Mount Zion.

In speaking of the different spheres or "mountains" of culture, we see that there are different elements that make up culture. Government, religion, arts, media, education, etc. are the building blocks of what defines a culture. These prophetic Scriptures speak to this same thing. We must allow men and women of God to carry His heart into places of influence, but it is even more important to give attention to this mountain where He dwells.

Scripture prophesies that in the last days the house of prayer, or Mount Zion, will be established above all other mountains. This is the place of His presence, and it shall take first priority above all the other spheres of culture.

\We are in these latter days, where the resting place of God's presence will be the exalted place that is raised above all other mountains and hills of culture. His presence will be the foremost and highest pursuit of all people. People from all nations will flow to it. Usually things flow down from the top of a mountain, yet here there is a flowing *to* the top of the mountain. In the Kingdom of God up is down and down is up. The foundational things are often the most important.

Atop Mount Zion people will learn the ways of God. They will be taught about the Lord and learn His ways. They will be obedient and walk in His paths, not learning the letter but the spirit of the law. Not learning mere knowledge to puff up our intellect, but learning the ways of God intimately and personally.

If we want to have influence just so people will hear what we think, we are in for a grave awakening. I don't want to ascend the hill of a sphere of culture; I want to ascend the hill of the Lord. Atop the hill of the Lord I can speak to all mountains and they will hear me.

God sends people to different spheres of culture to bring the kingdom of God, but blessed is the main whose heart is set on Zion. Blessed is the man or women whose heart is set upon the "one thing" (Psalm 27:4).

Daniel the prophet changed culture, but that wasn't his goal. He simply wanted to serve God and know His ways.

We make things too complex if we draw away from the simplicity of purity and devotion to Christ alone. The apostle Paul warned of this.

> "I am jealous for you with a godly jealousy. I promised you to one husband, to Christ, so that I might present you as a pure virgin to him. But I am afraid that just as Eve was deceived by the serpent's cunning, your minds may somehow be led astray from your sincere and pure devotion to Christ." (2 Corinthians 11:2–3)

Daniel's secret life is what got him into trouble. It wasn't the boisterous public displays of his religion, but his private devotion and dedication that changed an empire.

Daniel was devoted to God in his personal life. When charged to eat in a way that convicted his conscience before God, he refused. When commanded not to pray to any other gods but Nebuchadnezzar, he continued praying earnestly to God in his secret place, with the door shut behind him, three times a day. His private devotion made a way for God to use Daniel to make public exploits.

I heard Lou Engle once say that Daniel had influence in Babylon because Babylon didn't have influence inside of Daniel. This is true. Daniel fasted and prayed before God to have understanding. He cheated death in the lion's den because God honors those who honor Him.

If you honor God when no one is looking, He will honor you when everyone is looking!

After Daniel's divine protection from the lions, King

Nebuchadnezzar issued a decree from that Daniel's God was the only true God and that He alone was worthy to be worshipped!

> I issue a decree that in every part of my kingdom people must fear and reverence the God of Daniel. For He is the living God and He endures forever; His kingdom will not be destroyed, His dominion will never end. He rescues and he saves; He performs signs and wonders in the heavens and on the earth. He has rescued Daniel from the power of the lions. (Daniel 6:26–27)

Many times our small acts of devotion to God in secret cause others to do the talking while we simply do what we're called to do. If we will give our lives to the little things and live before God alone, we will turn the world upside down. Like Paul and Silas's songs and prayers in the prison, and Daniel's prayers in his room, the small acts of making Jesus King cause great shockwaves to be released, more than we may ever know!

Chapter 16

LIVING AHEAD
OF YOUR TIME AS PRIESTS

J esus spoke of David as a prototype of what it looks like to enter into the fullness of God. David is the atypical example of a wholehearted worshipper and yet a man with flaws like any other. God said he made David a leader and commander of the people to show them the way to a greater level of blessing than they had ever known (Isaiah 55:3-4).

Matthew 12:1-7 is perhaps one of the most compelling and incredible Scriptures I have ever read.

> At that time Jesus went through the grain fields on the Sabbath. And His disciples were hungry, and began to pluck heads of grain and to eat. And when the Pharisees saw it, they said to Him, "Look, Your disciples are doing what is not lawful to do on the Sabbath!"
>
> But He said to them, "Have you not read what David did when he was hungry, he and those who were with him: how he entered the house of God and ate the showbread which was not lawful for him to eat, nor for those who were with him, but only for the priests? Or have you not read in the law that on the Sabbath the priests in the

temple profane the Sabbath, and are blameless? Yet I say to you that in this place there is One greater than the temple. For the Son of Man is LORD of the Sabbath." (Matthew 12:1-7)

Jesus ends His discourse by revealing that these religious believers' gaze was on the law. They believed that the purpose of the law was to keep people in line. They were focused on what *could not* be done in God, but here Jesus brought focus to what *could* be done in God.

According to their religious rendering of the word of God, void of real revelation, the Pharisees accused Jesus of doing something unlawful. Jesus took this opportunity to give a glimpse into the realm of the impossible through the power of the eternal covenant. He brought to mind the time when David did something that only a priest could do. David was a king, yet he acted in a priestly role when he ate the showbread—the "bread of the presence," as they called it. Essentially Jesus said that David was not only a king, but a priest as well. He went on to exemplify the priestly privilege and said that even if the priests profaned the Sabbath day, or didn't act in perfect accordance with the law, they would still be blameless because of their position in God. He was saying that the priests had special rights. The priests were worshippers. Worshippers who love God have special privileges. The lovers of God don't follow rules; they follow the Spirit. They are not subject to religious precepts but to His Holy Spirit.

David had no understanding of what he was doing in his day from any previous person who was both a king and a priest. Except for one: Melchizedek.

For this Melchizedek, king of Salem, priest of the Most High God, who met Abraham as he was returning from the slaughter of the kings and blessed him. (Hebrews 7:1)

David was an old-covenant man living in new-covenant realities. He tapped into something that was before his time, something outside of time itself. The eternal covenant is acted upon by faith and through relationship to God. This is the eternal covenant spoken of in Hebrews 13:20, whereby the Lamb slain before time, before the foundations of the world, gave access to those who would walk with God in true love and intimacy. As a result, they could access possibilities not yet fully realized in their generation.

This was true of Enoch, who walked with God and didn't taste death but was taken by God. Jesus said that those who believed on Him would not see or taste death (John 11:26). Enoch truly lived this out. His walk with God sets a standard even for New Covenant believers. Enoch never died; he went on a walk with God and never came back! (Hebrews 11:5)

It was true of Phineas, who accessed the perpetual or continual and generational priesthood because he lived and walked in jealous love for his God and knew His heart. Because of Phineas' jealous love for God he was promised that all his generations after him would be priests (Numbers 25:1–12). That is the reward of living jealous for God, your sons and daughters will be priests!

This was true of David, who, because of a real relationship and a heart after God, was a forerunner and a foreshadowing of the new-covenant believer. God gave so much honor to David that He said that His Son would sit upon the throne of David. Jesus is even called the Son of David.

God is outside of time. There are places in God that can be accessed through relationship with Him, at His will and sovereignty, which defy natural laws.

David accessed the ancient, eternal priesthood order of Melchizedek. Melchizedek was the priest and king whom Abraham offered his tithe to. Hebrews 6:20 says that Jesus is a High Priest according to the order of Melchizedek. This is a place of friendship with God by which we can access promises in the word not yet fully realized in a corporate setting. Jesus told us to pray that the kingdom of God would come to earth. He did not put a limit on the amount of ground we could gain, individually or corporately. Pioneers are called to go places no one else has gone. An enormous part of being a pioneer of the presence is going places in relationship with God so as to make a way for others to follow that it may become a new normal.

Hebrews chapter 6 speaks of "tasting of the power of the age to come." We should be tasting and seeing promises of the age to come; it is our inheritance. Inheritance isn't for when we die. It's for us while we're alive, because someone who loved us and left us this inheritance died. The exploits of all the men and women of the Bible and of church history will come upon us as well.

The friends of God in this generation will do things that will make the religious spit and devils quit. They will make kings wonder and put hell asunder. All of heaven and the great cloud of witnesses wait with bated breath to see if we will access the untold power that lies within every born-again believer. We don't know what we have. Oh, that the mysteries and riches would be unveiled in this generation!

The religious spirit puts limitations on our walk with God, just as the Pharisees did with Jesus. Jesus frees us to limitless possibilities. Our walk with Him can produce results beyond our wildest imagination.

God does establish boundaries for our safety. Even in the paradise and freedom of the garden of Eden, there were boundaries. We must never seek God for any other reason than to know Him and be submitted to His will. Peter died a martyr's death, yet the apostle John did not have a recorded death date. Jesus is God, and God can do anything He pleases, whether it fits in our box or not. We all have different destinies, yet we should all press into Him in the uttermost way and follow Him no matter what our fate or calling may be.

We, as priests, are of the order of Melchizedek. We are of an eternal and unending priesthood whose primary identity is as worshippers and ministers of God. As kings, we exercise influence in the earth to bring about God's will, purpose, and plan.

We are heavenly people. Citizens of the kingdom of heaven who are pilgrims passing through this earthly realm with varying assignments, all with the singular focus of taking dominion and making Jesus King.

Identity as Priests

> Prove yourselves doers of the word, and not merely hearers who delude themselves. For if anyone is a hearer of the word and not a doer, he is like a man who looks at his natural face in a mirror; for once he has looked at himself and gone away, he has immediately forgotten what kind of person he was. (James 1:22–24)

Identity is important. It is vital that we know and remember who we are. James says that those who hear the word of God and don't do it are like those who look in a mirror only to turn away and forget who they are. When you don't know who you are, you won't do what you were made to do. When you don't do what you have heard from the Word of God, you lose your identity. This is how we become "mirror dwellers," living life always looking in the mirror. We call those who are constantly looking at themselves in the mirror *vain*. And vanity is selfishness.

Spiritual vanity stunts the progress of our growth in God because we are constantly seeking the next word, the next big speaker, the next "new thing." This is vain and selfish because we haven't done the first things we were told. We become self-obsessed instead of self-less. We look into the Word and see our identity, but if we fail to practice walking out our identity, we deceive ourselves.

Jesus said that when we come to Him, hear His word, and do it, we become like those who dug, laid a foundation, and then built a house upon it. Many of us are guilty of doing two-thirds of this. We come and we hear, but don't actually do. When the storms of life come, we are found desolate, and our unfinished "house" is revealed.

> "Why do you call Me, 'Lord, Lord,' and do not do what I say?" Everyone who comes to Me and hears My words and acts on them, I will show you whom he is like: he is like a man building a house, who dug deep and laid a foundation on the rock; and when a flood occurred, the torrent burst against that house and could not shake it, because it had been well built. "But the one who has heard and has not acted accordingly, is like a man who built a house on the ground without any foundation; and the torrent burst against it and immediately it collapsed, and the ruin of that house was great." (Luke 6:46–49)

We are many things in our relationship to God. We are sheep, and He is our Shepherd. We are sons and daughters, and He the

Father. We are servants, and He is the Master. He is the General, and we are the army. We are the bride, and He is the bridegroom.

There is a corresponding revelation and breakthrough for us associated with each of these relational truths. The Bible declares in Revelation 5:10 that we are kings and priests to our God.

First Peter 2:5 says we are a royal priesthood. Our kingship and our priesthood go hand in hand. King David was a king and a priest. He operated as both. This is a primary truth we must receive in order to understand our role in this current time. God is turning our identity from ministers to people first, into ministers to Him first. There is a divine order, and when we do it differently than how He has designed it to be, we will not see the results the Bible promises. Priests gain authority in the spiritual and use that authority in the natural as kings.

Priests minister to God. They stand between God and man. Their calling is as friends of God who represent Him to the earth. God's original intention was that Israel be a nation of priests and kings to the rest of the earth.

> "You shall be to Me a kingdom of priests and a holy nation." These are the words that you shall speak to the sons of Israel. (Exodus 19:6)

We are now the new-creation people, whose primary identity is as priests to God.

Priests were the only ones who could carry God's presence. David learned this when he brought the ark of the covenant, which was the literal representation of God's presence on earth, back into Jerusalem.

The Philistines built an ox cart to carry the Presence. But the presence of the living God could not be carried on things built by man. Only the priests could do that, and only upon their shoulders.

The same is true today. The world yearns for the presence of the living God, whether they know it or not. As the church, our greatest initiatives and appeals to the world will not bring the presence of God to them. Only as priests can we carry His glory so they may taste and see that the Lord is good.

We must be the house of prayer. We must build the tabernacle of David. Jesus declares today to all new-covenant believers that His house will be called a house of prayer, just as He did in His earthly ministry when He drove out the compromise in the temple, quoting Isaiah 56:7:

> "Even those I will bring to My holy mountain (Zion), and make them joyful in My house of prayer. Their burnt offerings and their sacrifices will be acceptable on My altar; For my house will be called a house of prayer for all the peoples."

Our identity and primary function is as priests of our God. He lives in us, not in buildings. We are His house, and we must be embodied and defined as a people and place of communion with our God.

In Luke 4:18–19, Jesus picked up a scroll to read the Scriptures. He read Isaiah 61, which reads, in part, "The Spirit of The Lord is upon me, because He has anointed me."

Jesus then sat down and told the congregation, "Today this scripture has been fulfilled in your hearing." He made a vast and sweeping declaration that what Isaiah prophesied about had come to pass. He made the compelling and daring proclamation that He was the Messiah, the Christ, the Anointed One.

If Isaiah 61 was fulfilled in Jesus, we have to read this as a promise for what we are called and able to walk in. Jesus said that He came to fulfill all the Law and the Prophets. In Him and the new covenant, we can walk in all the promises of God that are shown in the Word of God. Jesus is the *yes* and *amen* to God's promises. Let's read a little further in Isaiah 61. Verses 4 and 6 refer to the believer:

> They will rebuild the ancient ruins, they will raise up the former devastations; and they will repair the ruined cities, the desolations of many generations. ... But you will be called the priests of the LORD; you will be spoken of as ministers of our God. (Isaiah 61:4–6)

We will restore the earth. We will repair ruined cities and restore the desolations of many generations. How? Through the priesthood.

Verse 6 tells us how we will be known to the earth. People will say, "Who rebuilt cities and restored ancient ruins of generations?" And the answer will be, "They are the *priest* of God Almighty, *they are those who minister to God.*"

Priests who bring His presence will turn desolate regions into beautiful habitations. The priesthood of the believer must arise in a real way. We must be known as people who are worshippers first and foremost, who pray night and day for our cities. Christians have been known as many things: haters, bigots, religious, perhaps even those who do good deeds. But when our primary identity to the world and all around us proclaims, "Those are the worshipers and ministers of God," whole cities, regions, and generations will be rebuilt and restored!

We will see the earth returned to a garden. Not by the hardest workers, but by the faithful lovers of God. Isaiah 51:3 says:

"Indeed the LORD will comfort Zion; He will comfort all her waste places. And her wilderness He will make like Eden. And her desert like the garden of The Lord."

Zion is the homeland of the priests of God. They will make a garden for God to walk in once again. Let us arise as priests, and with our worship and prayer make a landing pad and dwelling place for God Almighty to come.

Press into God today. Build altars of His presence in your towns and cities. Make an environment of His glory known so that products of that environment come forth. Jesus made it clear that those who know God and who tap into this priesthood will do things that defy the age they live in. Let us be those who change nations with the simplicity of worship, prayer, and the priesthood.

Chapter 17

PRESENCE PIONEERS

Pioneering a place where God is comfortable begins inwardly and ends outwardly. We cannot build something in our homes or cities if we have not first built a place in our own lives for Him. You can teach what you know, but you can only impart who you are. Impartation is necessary for transformation. We can build schools of thought around a philosophy of His presence. We can have people believe things in their head about the presence of God. But unless we carry His presence in our lives, we cannot impart the reality or manifestation of the change people need. We cannot settle a place for God's presence in our cities if we have not settled the territory of our own hearts in Him.

Are we so proud and haughty to think we can go to the hardest and darkest regions of the world and see change when we haven't conquered the hardness and darkness of our own hearts? The hardest and darkest place on earth is our own desires that have not been crucified. Even Jesus had to labor in prayer to lay down any desires of His will that were contrary to the Father's plan. He won this battle in Gethsemane so He could have the victory on Calvary.

We must cultivate our hearts as gardens where God dwells. We must give heed to the secret place where only He hears our worship and prayers. This is the key to sustained and eternal breakthrough. The unseen things are eternal, but the seen things will fade away. If all of your worship and prayer is in the seen places, what do you think will become of your work in the long haul?

We must carry authority as a personal lifestyle. It means nothing if we have all the talk and none of the walk. True authority to plant cultures of God's presence in the earth comes from pioneers who carry the DNA of His presence. <u>You can only reproduce that which you are.</u> If we carry the inward flame of devotion to God, we will reproduce people who carry the fire of His presence. We are called to live from the overflow of our walk with Him.

A measure of His presence exists in all places and at all times. After all, the earth is the Lord's and the fullness thereof (Psalm 24:1). However, though God is in all believers, His Spirit is not given full freedom to manifest itself in its fullness on all believers. A lifestyle of surrender to the Holy Spirit will open up the door for more of Him to be experienced by others. So will you go to hell if you don't do this? No. But others may!

I am not talking here about salvation or the eternal state of our souls. You do not have to carry God's presence to get into heaven. But if you don't, you are robbing the world of an encounter with God through you. The world is crying out for a real encounter with God.

Our "Romans Road" and "sinner's prayer" have perhaps sent more people to a hellish life without God than all the demons in hell because they downplay the importance of an encounter with God for salvation. Instead we reason it into a decision of the mind, an ascent of the intellect to certain truths. God has to be in the equation of salvation. Salvation is not possible without the work of the Holy Spirit. Just because we get someone to say a prayer does not mean they are born-again in Christ.

I do not intend to demean the work of many well-meaning and pure-hearted Christians. Nor am I saying that all of these works have been in vain. God gives greater grace! But we cannot rely on programs and good purpose alone. We must have His presence. God is moving us from the purpose-driven church into the presence-driven church. When we are provoked by His love, we will carry the overflow of that encounter everywhere we go for those who need it.

We are more than robots, talking people into believing something as foolish and crazy as Christ crucified. We are walking, living conduits of a God encounter!

The more I preach the simple, straight gospel to people wherever I am, the more I realize the need for the Holy Spirit's power and presence to be evident. A heartless repetition of words cannot save anyone.

I have seen both of my children's births, and let me tell you, being born is not a walk in the park. It is an intense miracle! The harvest is ripe. People are longing for Jesus, whether they know it or not. How can we tell them about a God we don't really know ourselves?

When we do evangelism or purposeful street ministry backed by prayer and worship over a certain place or person, the results are night-and-day different from evangelism without prayer and worship. I have seen this time and time again. The presence of God breaks through the hard places and prepares the ground for His word to be planted. The presence of God makes ministry easy! This is why when the church on earth begins to look like the church in heaven—offering up hours of nonstop worship and prayer in churches and cities all over the world, the number of salvations, healings, and miracles are always ten times the amount they were before the presence of God was made priority.

The presence of God among us and upon us changes the game. We go from those who know about God to those who know God. We go from those who speak from what they know to those who know of whom they speak. There is a vast difference.

One of the most notable differences in the ministry of Jesus was when He spoke. Throughout His entire earthly ministry, people marveled at the power of His words. They said He spoke with authority. They said, "No one has ever spoke like this" (John 7:46). They noticed because all their lives they had only heard the Pharisees and other religious folk, who spoke with no true authority.

People can tell the difference between words with authority and words with no authority.

Jesus was filled with the Spirit before He went into the wilderness, but when He returned, He came in the power of the Holy Spirit.

I have seen the difference between words with the power and presence of God behind them and words that are void of any real life and power—in others and in my own ministry. Many Christians sing in worship, and God faithfully comes. But God sings out of only a few. Many preach and teach from their giftings. But few speak with the authority of Almighty God behind it.

This is also true in a corporate sense. Any person who is in tune with the spiritual climate of a place can tell you that different cities and nations feel different. Some friends of mine just completed a journey, going through every county in my state and releasing worship, praise, and prayer. They told me they could drive into a certain geographical regions and "feel" the darkness. Upon studying, they found that this area had been home to much injustice and poverty. The fruit of the darkness in the spiritual could be clearly seen.

They then drove just one county over and said it felt as if someone had turned on a light switch. They felt light and hopeful, and the ease of perceiving the goodness of God flooded the car. As they came into the town where they were to worship, they spotted a House of Prayer. They went to greet the people there and struck up a conversation with the man who oversaw that house of prayer, and he informed them that they had been praying and worshipping faithfully over their region for six to seven years. You can feel the difference when the presence of God is not manifest in a place!

We need the presence of God in the dark places of the earth. If we emphasize the presence of God in all we do in our towns, cities, and regions, new churches will spring up, anointed preaching will come forth, souls will be saved, and justice will speedily come (Luke 18).

I am not talking about the next new cool thing here. I am not advocating that what is being said has the monopoly on all things God can do to change cities. I am merely a servant who wants to see the body of Christ be blessed by the Presence. I want to see cities changed and blessed because of the presence of God within it. What the presence touches will change! It is not the only thing, but it is the first thing.

Chapter 18

MONASTIC MISSIONARIES

A new breed of missionary is arising. One who will be sent by the Holy Spirit and commissioned by the church to take the gospel of Jesus to the edge of the world, into the darkest and hardest places. What sets apart these new fiery-eyed missionaries is their focus. While the thrust of missions in the last hundred years has been making conversions and saving souls, the new missionary has a different focus, yet achieves the same ultimate result.

Of course we want souls to be saved. Of course we want to see people receive Christ who have never heard His name. We should earnestly desire to teach people the ways of Jesus. This is the commission of Christ to the church: to make disciples. Jesus taught His disciples to follow Him much like God taught the children of Israel to follow His presence in the wilderness out of Egypt. There is no question that Jesus has called His church to go. But as God is intertwining the revelation of prayer and missions, we have to change our idea of what *going* looks like.

What we have missed, perhaps, is the idea of *how* we go and *what* we're going for.

> He said to his disciples, "The harvest is plentiful, but the laborers are few; therefore pray earnestly to the Lord of

the harvest to send out laborers into his harvest." (Matthew 9:37–38)

Jesus taught His disciples how to pray for the harvest before telling them to go into the harvest. Prayer changes everything. Co-laboring with God in prayer is the heartbeat of the Lord's deep desire for intimacy. Co-laboring is the key to completing the Great Commission.

In the past we have said that some go into the mission field and others pray. In part I believe this to be true. There is, however, a group of people who embody the fullness of God's heart in this matter. They will *pray and go.*

Throughout church history, we have seen a monastic expression of following Christ: monks and or nuns who have separated themselves from the world in order to give themselves to prayer and service of Christ in complete isolation from other people. The introversion of this lifestyle is the opposite of the typical missionary lifestyle. Missionaries are mostly typified by giving their lives away to others and spend every waking moment serving people and laboring for conversion among unreached people groups.

To Go and Be Sent

At the beginning of chapter 13 in the book of Acts, there is an important biblical principle that I call the "Antioch Principle." God is not one of formulas, but He is one of principles. Formulas have a tendency to evade true intimacy and real relationship, while principles are boundaries and truths that actually enhance healthy relationship.

> Now there were at Antioch, in the church that was there, prophets and teachers: Barnabas, and Simeon who was called Niger, and Lucius of Cyrene, and Manaen who had

been brought up with Herod the tetrarch, and Saul. While they were ministering to the Lord and fasting, the Holy Spirit said, "Set apart for Me Barnabas and Saul for the work to which I have called them." Then, when they had fasted and prayed and laid their hands on them, they sent them away. So, being sent out by the Holy Spirit, they went down to Seleucia and from there they sailed to Cyprus. (Acts 13:1-4)

The believers in Antioch were ministering, worshipping, and fasting unto the Lord. They were in a time of "priesting" before God and living out this first-commandment lifestyle. The Holy Spirit called out Paul and Barnabas from the place of ministering to God.

God wants to call out sent ones from the prayer room rather than the boardroom. Human wisdom and knowledge pick out those we deem most capable to do a job. God sees differently. The prophet Samuel would have picked one of King David's brothers by his own intuition, yet God chose the one who wasn't even invited to the party, little David out in the shepherd field.

It is not our job to choose who does what; it is God's job. How can we know unless we are found in the place of prayer and ministering unto Him?

While Paul and Barnabas were ministering in Antioch, the Holy Spirit decided to "set apart Barnabas and Paul for the work to which I have called them." God calls us from the place of intimacy to do His work.

I never imagined God would use me the way He has, yet from the place of intimacy and ministering unto Him I have seen God launch me and many others into the works we were called to do.

The church in Antioch bore witness to what the Holy Spirit was doing with Paul and Barnabas, and so the church leaders commissioned them with the laying on of hands. They blessed them and affirmed that the Holy Spirit was sending them.

God has put the church in our lives for us, not to be against us. Leaders should recognize when God is doing something, even if it goes against what they think is right. We should bless what God is doing.

The church of Antioch saw that God had called these two men to missionary work. Paul and Barnabas had both the witness of God and the witness of the church. When we are called to go, God wants the church to send us. He wants to launch sons and daughters into missionary works, not see rejected orphans fly off to the nations like feathers in the wind.

While people have had to obey the call of God without the support and blessing of their church leaders, we must lay hold of this revelation and do things the way God intended it. Let us call the children of God back to the place of intimacy. God loves the expression of houses of prayer, worship furnaces (places of extended worship and prayer to keep the fire burning on the altar that Leviticus 6:12–13 describes), and prioritizing ministering to God through worship and prayer in our meetings.

God sends us from the place of living out the first commandment to fulfill the second commandment.

The churches today that follow the Antioch principle emphasize ministering to God first. Because of this, many are being launched into cities and nations across the earth. These launched ones are carrying the seal of the Holy Spirit's calling with the blessing of the church behind them.

Monastic Missionaries

In the past, there has been a polarization of the monastic lifestyle of seclusion and the missionary lifestyle of nonstop ministry to people. Today, God is doing both.

Jesus told us to go, but what do we do when we get where we're going?

God wants monastic missionaries who exemplify a lifestyle of intimacy and who minister to others from the overflow of their relationship with Him. God wants missionaries to build a resting place for Him in unreached lands. The tabernacle of David is being rebuilt to restore first love to the church while simultaneously giving the world a face-to-face encounter with God and His life-changing presence and glory.

Missionary burnout and ministry burnout occur when the flame in our lamps simply goes out. When the oil is gone, the flame dies. This happens when people's primary concern is ministry to people rather than ministry to God.

We must build a place for the Presence. What good is it to be sent from the place of intimacy with God into a place where we "gain the whole world" but lose our first love?

Missionaries must contend for breakthrough in the heavens. Priestly workers must contend in prayer and worship before trying to win souls. Souls will come and the nations will receive the Lord when they see His beauty. The tabernacle of David displays the manifest presence and glory of God, both upon the believer and in entire geographical locations. Jesus is beautiful, and God longs for His Son to be put on display in the place of worship and prayer.

Are we so satisfied with the wine of the past that we don't want to hear about what God is pouring out now? I believe in the power of preaching the simple good news of Christ and Him crucified, but we must do so in power, not in word only. A powerless preacher in dark nations filled with blinded people is useless. Shining ones must come out of the secret place with God to declare and manifest who Jesus is through signs, wonders, miracles, and the reality of carrying the presence of the one of whom they speak.

The nations will come to the presence of God in the same way the jailer came to Paul and Silas in the prison (Acts 16:30–31). The jailer came to the Presence and asked what many people, tribes, and tongues ask: "What must I do to be saved?"

> After this I will return and *rebuild David's fallen tent*. Its ruins I will rebuild, and I will restore it, *that the rest of mankind may seek the Lord*, even all the Gentiles who bear my name, says the Lord, who does these things. (Acts 15:16–17)

Pray and Go. Go and pray. Worship and go. Go and worship.

This is the call to the monastic missionaries—monks who set themselves apart in the furnace of intimacy and explode into the streets, just like the believers in Acts 2 in the upper room. There, the Bible says, "People came to the sound" (Acts 2:6).

People are coming to the sound of worship! We have never seen what is about to happen. A harvest is going to be caught up in the net of God's presence like never before. We can't even totally describe what is coming on the corporate level because we've never seen it. We have biblical precedence for it, but no modern history has recorded the massive number of people who are about to be saved and discipled in the presence of God.

Before the flood, Noah had never seen rain. Imagine God telling you to build something because of something coming you had never heard of or seen. God is telling "Noahs" to build places of the presence of God in their families, their communities, and their nations for a massive harvest the likes of which has never been seen. We stand on the cusp of breakthrough. The rain is about to fall as a flood of prodigals and unbelievers come. From the homosexual community to the atheistic propagators, from the Muslims to the Buddhists, all are about to see the beauty of Jesus and experience the power of His presence!

Chapter 19

THE BABY AMONG US

Many in this generation were raised on Hot Pockets and high-speed Internet. Our understanding of how long things take to develop can be skewed. However, having experienced second-hand how long it takes for a child to develop during the nine months of pregnancy, I've learned there are certain things that simply can't be rushed. I watched my precious wife grow, with grace, to deliver both of our children full term. But even after all that, a newborn is completely helpless, absolutely and utterly dependent upon the mother. A newborn cannot lift his own head. He cannot take care of himself in any capacity. He can't even tell you what he wants other than by crying.

With this experience fresh in my mind, the Lord showed me how His kingdom operates. Perfect praise is found in nursing babes and infants. A life that offers up perfect praise is as dependent on God as a nursing infant.

We tend to expect God to show up immediately and fully. And while God does do "suddenlys," these are usually preceded by many unseen things building up to that point. His kingdom is like a seed; it starts out small and grows into a large tree. It's like a little leaven hidden inside a lump of dough that works its way out. The kingdom of God is an inner reality that works its way to the outer. The spiritual kingdom works its way into the natural, starting small and seemingly insignificant, then growing into something large and noticeable.

The greatest move of God of all time came as a small, helpless baby, born in a barn because there was no other place available. This mighty revival of all revivals came into the world unable to talk or eat on His own. He was completely dependent on others to take care of him. He was born in the most undesirable and unsanitary places you could imagine. God Himself was born into humble circumstances in every respect. And Jesus grew up like a normal person, in a human body, subject to the earth and those He created.

This move of God grew up before the eyes of the very ones who'd prayed for it. The Pharisees, the religious elite of their day, with doctrines and diplomas in hand, had prayed with more religious fervor than anyone else for the Messiah to come. And they had figured out exactly *how* the Messiah would come. They watched the answer to their prayers grow up right under their noses. Yet when Jesus' ministry was revealed in its fullness, they rejected Him. In John 5:39, Jesus said:

> You search the scriptures for in them you think you have eternal life, but you refuse to come to me that you may have life. (John 5:39)

Jesus was the Word of God made flesh, and they didn't recognize Him. Their god was doctrine and dogma, and that blinded their eyes to see what God was doing. They knew the Bible, but not the God of the Bible.

Those who pray most fervently for God to move are the very ones at risk of crucifying the precious gift when it comes. We who pray for revival are often the first to kill it because it does not fit in line with what we had in mind. Our expectations take precedence over our anticipation. We put guidelines on our expectations of what it will look like when God answers our prayers for revival.

Don't be deceived. Revival is common looking. Yet if we place our guidelines around it, it will be offensive and dangerous to our ideals. We must remain zealous in prayer while being childlike so as to see Him when He comes. Only the little children can see the kingdom of God.

Only the humble ones recognized Jesus as a baby. Anna the prophetess had given her life to fasting and prayer. She lived a life of intimacy with God. This oil of intimacy in her lamp gave her light to see what others couldn't. Having nothing to do with outward signs, she recognized the Messiah by revelation and the illumination of God's Spirit upon Him.

With the light of God's presence, people can see things they would otherwise pass by. The prophets of today will see what God is doing if their lamps are filled with the oil of His presence through lifestyles of intimacy with God, typified by prayer and worship.

The current move of God on the earth is in its infancy. We can see prophetically much of what it is going to do, but we cannot know in full just how powerful it will be.

This revival is *here* and it is *coming*. We have a measure of breakthrough, but there is more to be had. Jesus told the Samaritan woman, "A time is *here* and is now *coming* when worshipers will worship in spirit and truth" ([REFERENCE], emphasis added). Jesus spoke from outside of time, from the place of eternity.

Christ is in us now, as is the kingdom of God, yet Christ and His kingdom are also coming. Revival is here and there is more on the way!

Much like Jesus growing up before the people of His day, this move of God, this habitation of the Lord's presence, will grow up before us. Jesus was the living fulfillment of the tabernacle of David. He lived thirty-three years on earth, the same amount of time the tent of David hosted the resting place of God's Spirit on the earth, whom all could see and experience. Jesus introduced this way of hosting God's presence and made it the standard for every believer. We are in a revival of the presence of God. It is being hosted by many people, cities, and nations. It will continue to grow, and its full power has yet to be seen. We can enjoy the current move of God while simultaneously hungering and praying for more of God's plan and fullness to come.

When Jesus came to earth, He was the fullness of God in the form of man. Jesus was and is the God-Man. Yet Jesus grew. The fullness of God grew! Not only did He physically grow, but from the age of twelve Jesus grew in favor and stature with God and man. The revealing of Jesus' public ministry was the climax of God's purpose, leading all the way to the cross. God the Son grew in favor with God the Father. We too are always growing. We never arrive.

Revival and *awakening* are two terms that describe the moving of God on the earth, whether that be in the church, in the world, or both.

God uses the prayers of His people to bring forth His plans and purposes on the earth. Therefore, we should unashamedly pray for revival. Without our prayers the fullness can't come. When we understand the amazing time we are living in, while also comprehending the great privilege of prayer to usher in the greater things God wishes to do in the earth, we will be a joyful bride!

What happens when church prayer meetings, houses of prayer, and worship furnaces have been going strong for fifty years? What happens when the second and third generations after us are raised in a culture of worship and prayer, the presence of God, and a first-commandment lifestyle? Amos 9:11 and Acts 15:16 declare that the rebuilding of David's tabernacle will cause the nations to come to know God.

A mighty harvest like we've never dreamed is coming. Heaven will invade the earth. The greater things we pray for will be fulfilled in the generations of believers who come after us. This is the wise plan of God. When we think multigenerational, we understand that God is doing something in our day like never before.

There have been restorations of the tabernacle of David before. But what we are living in now is a new thing. Never before in history have houses of prayer sprung up like they are currently. Worship is hijacking church services across the world. People are hungering for God and His presence in a global way that demands our attention. It is as if the restoration project of David's tabernacle on the earth is in overhaul! Hundreds of prayer rooms are popping up all over the globe. God is up to something! It's as if we are reaching a deadline and production is at maximum speed.

I had the privilege of hosting a nonstop prayer and worship room at a major Christian conference. Some of the world's top worship groups and artists were present. Many of today's most well-known and powerful leaders were also there. This three-day event drew more than eighty thousand people. My job was to have a prayer and worship room for the duration of the conference. We were in a side room inside the huge arena.

The first day, the presence of God descended upon us in such a weighty way that when people walked into the room, they could barely stand.

The next day, the small room, which only held about 250 people, was packed, and we had a long line. A huge group stood outside the doors, waiting to get in, wanting to be close to the glory. I assumed that once the big-name worship groups and speakers took the stage, the room would clear out. But people had been hijacked by the presence of God and couldn't leave!

Hundreds of people were lit on fire during that event to do something similar in their hometowns. Still today I visit places that were sparked to host God's presence by catching the heart of what God is doing in this generation.

God's presence is being prioritized in the church like never before. God is wooing His church to their first love, and He does not apologize for it. Those who peer with disgust on this movement will be as Michel, King David's wife. She looked down from her high place and saw David dancing wildly before the Lord's presence and was embarrassed that a king would act in such a way. Her disdain for worship led her to become barren.

God wants to birth many dreams into the earth, and He will do it through the womb of Zion, which is the epitome of intimacy. Intimacy bears children. Those who do not sing along to God's song in the earth in this day will not bring forth children. They will find it difficult to bear fruit, especially fruit that remains. The dreams of God and the destinies of people will die sterile in their worship-less wombs unless they sing!

> "Shout for joy, O barren one, you who have borne no child; break forth into joyful shouting and cry aloud, you who have not travailed; for the sons of the desolate one will be more numerous than the sons of the married woman," says the LORD. (Isaiah 54:1)

Months and years of not seeing what God is doing has robbed us of the faith, hope, and perseverance we need to press on. Many great leaders and faithful laborers have given up or moved on to other things because of a lack of sight, or lack of godly perspective. No one has the full picture; we all see in part. But we can know what the Lord is doing in every season of life. If we are not seeing that, perhaps our lamps aren't bright enough.

Many have traded following the presence of God for following good ideas and the wisdom of men, because their lamps have grown dim and they can no longer see the narrow path. If your lamp is dim, your oil is low. If you're running on fumes, it's time to get some fuel so you can have proper perspective again.

"At that time the kingdom of heaven will be like ten virgins who took their lamps and went out to meet the bridegroom. Five of them were foolish and five were wise. The foolish ones took their lamps but did not take any oil with them. The wise ones, however, took oil in jars along with their lamps. The bridegroom was a long time in coming, and they all became drowsy and fell asleep.

"At midnight the cry rang out: 'Here's the bridegroom! Come out to meet him!'

"Then all the virgins woke up and trimmed their lamps. The foolish ones said to the wise, 'Give us some of your oil; our lamps are going out.'

" 'No,' they replied, 'there may not be enough for both us and you. Instead, go to those who sell oil and buy some for yourselves.'

"But while they were on their way to buy the oil, the bridegroom arrived. The virgins who were ready went in with him to the wedding banquet. And the door was shut.

"Later the others also came. 'Lord, Lord,' they said, 'open the door for us!'

"But he replied, 'Truly I tell you, I don't know you.'" (Matthew 25:1–12)

This parable is talking about believers. Five of them were wise because they carried extra oil. Five were unwise because they only carried enough oil for the short term. The oil here speaks of the intimacy of God that gives fuel to our flame and light to our lamps. When some says, "Awake, the bridegroom comes," only the ones with extra oil are able to go with the bridegroom to the wedding banquet. The five unwise virgins asked for the other virgins' oil, to which they replied, basically, "It doesn't work that way!"

You can impart fire, but you cannot impart oil.

Oil comes from relationship with Jesus. The name of Jesus is like oil poured out (Song of Solomon 1:3), and there are no shortcuts to real relationship. The ones with oil, whose lamps are bright and shining, will be able to participate in the awakening, while the ones who only have enough oil to get by from day to day will be left out of experiencing the fullness they could have had.

When the unprepared believers knock on the door, they will hear from the Lord these sobering words: "I don't know you." This Scripture has many theological implications that have far-reaching truths. But undeniably present in this parable is the Lord's call for His people to have oil in their lamps. Not just oil that gets us by, but oil that overflows. Jesus admonishes us to live from the overflow of intimacy and relationship with Him. Many have lamps and many have ministries. But we must have ministries and lamps that are filled with the oil that comes from intimacy with God. The oil of intimacy fuels our lamps so that we may give light to others.

There is a baby among us. Awakening is here! It may look small and insignificant, hardly able to hold up its head, but its strength is only being seen in part. Many are pioneering places of prayer, worship, and the presence of God in their homes and towns across the earth in these days. We must constantly be filled with God's oil of intimacy to keep our hands on the plow of what we're doing. We cannot lose if we don't give up. Victory is ours if we do not grow weary in doing well.

We are building something today that will remain even after the coming of Christ. What is being built cannot be destroyed by human hands. The Spirit of God is stirring His church to make the earth a habitation for the presence and glory of God. May we say "Yes!" The Spirit and the Bride say, "Come! Even so, Lord, come!"

Printed in Poland
by Amazon Fulfillment
Poland Sp. z o.o., Wrocław